RIGBY

On Our Way
to English®

Unit Progress Tests

Grade 5

Rigby®

HOUGHTON MIFFLIN HARCOURT

www.Rigby.com
800-531-5015

Table of Contents

Overview of Unit Progress Tests

On Our Way to English Unit Progress Tests are designed to measure student progress in four key domains:

Vocabulary

- Provides sample and multiple-choice questions
- Assesses students' mastery of content-area vocabulary

Grammar

- Provides sample and multiple-choice questions
- Assesses students' mastery of grammar necessary to academic success

Reading

- Provides theme-related reading passages
- Assesses students' mastery of comprehension strategies and literacy skills

Writing

- Provides graphic organizer and related sample student writing
- Assesses students on the relationship between a graphic organizer used to plan writing and its subsequent piece of writing
- Assesses students on basic writing conventions

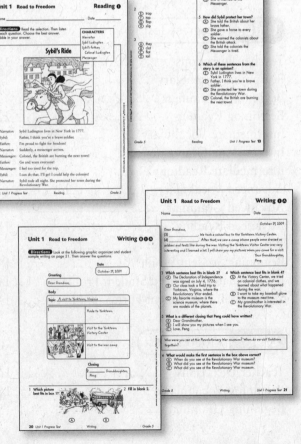

Unit Progress Test Levels

The Unit Progress Tests are provided at three levels—Beginning, Intermediate, Advanced. The test level students take depends on their Stage of Language Acquisition at the time the test is administered.

ⓑ Beginning Level   **Stage 1 or 2** (Preproduction or Early Production)

ⓘ Intermediate Level   **Stage 3** (Speech Emergence)

ⓐ Advanced Level   **Stage 4 or 5** (Intermediate Fluency or Advanced Fluency)

VOCABULARY LEVELS ●

Each level of the Vocabulary section of the tests has varying degrees of picture support and teacher scripting to meet English language learners at their Stage of Language Acquisition.

Beginning

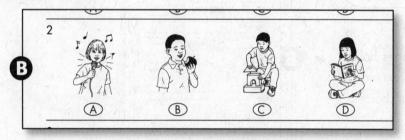

Intermediate

Advanced

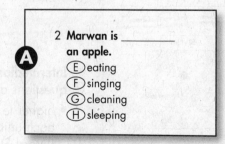

GRAMMAR LEVELS ·

Beginning questions assess students on grammar points taught to Stages 1–2 in the unit.

Intermediate and **Advanced** questions assess students on grammar points taught to Stages 3–5 in the unit.

I

1 Joseph likes music.
He _____ very well.
Ⓐ singing
Ⓑ sings
Ⓒ sing
Ⓓ not sing

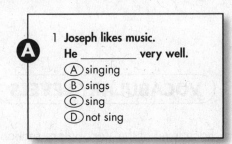

A

1 Joseph likes music.
He _____ very well.
Ⓐ singing
Ⓑ sings
Ⓒ sing
Ⓓ not sing

READING LEVELS ·

Beginning passages have
• strong picture-text match.
• picture answer choices.

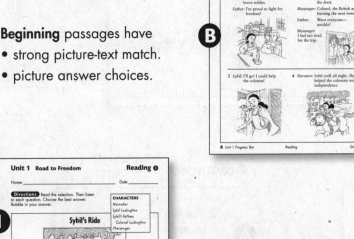

B

Intermediate and **Advanced** questions assess students on
• higher text level mastery of each unit's reading skills (Word Study, Comprehension Strategy, Literary Analysis, and Nonfiction Text Feature).

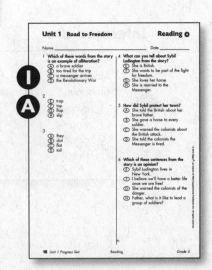

T4 *Unit Progress Tests*   Unit Progress Test Levels   *Grade 5*

Beginning English language learners are tested on item 1 only.

Intermediate and **Advanced** students complete both pages and are tested on

- their understanding of the relationship between a graphic organizer and its related writing piece.
- their mastery of writing conventions.

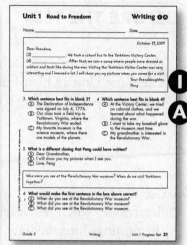

Writing Assessment Throughout *On Our Way to English*

By assessing the writing process skills taught in the unit, the Writing section of the Unit Progress Tests complements other Thematic Unit writing assessments. As the chart below shows, the Unit Progress Tests Writing section, the student writing piece gathered for each End-of-Unit Assessment in the Teacher's Guide, and Writing Self-Assessment on pages 77–78 of the Writing Resource Guide provide teachers information about all phases of the writing process to get a full picture of strengths and weaknesses.

	Writing Assessment Tool		
Skill Tested	Unit Progress Test Writing Section	Student Writing Piece	Writing Self-Assessment
Ability to Analyze/Understand Purpose of Graphic Organizers	•	•	•
Ability to Label Graphic Organizers	•	•	•
Ability to Use Graphic Organizers	•	•	
Student Reflection on Writing Ability			•
Message and Content	•	•	
Conventions of English	•	•	
Word Choice and Academic Language	•	•	
Fluency and Sentence Structure	•		

Test Administration

BEFORE THE TEST ·

1. The last week of each unit, determine students' Stages of Language Acquisition using the Thematic Unit's Open-Ended Oral Language Assessment and the Oral Language Rubric on pages A19–A34 of this book.

2. Use the following chart to determine which test level (Beginning, Intermediate, or Advanced) should be administered to each student.

Language Acquisition Stage	Unit Test Level
Stage 1 Preproduction	**B** Beginning
Stage 2 Early Production	**B** Beginning
Stage 3 Speech Emergence	**I** Intermediate
Stage 4 Intermediate Fluency	**A** Advanced
Stage 5 Advanced Fluency	**A** Advanced

3. List students who will test in the Beginning group and those who will test in the Intermediate/Advanced group. Students in the Beginning group should be assessed together and students in the Intermediate/Advanced group should be assessed together.

TESTING GROUPS ·

Beginning

- Pull Beginning English language learners into a small group and administer tests.
- Teacher Directions are designed to be read aloud to accommodate Beginning English language learners.

Intermediate and Advanced

- Pull Intermediate and Advanced English language learners into a small group and administer Intermediate and Advanced tests together in one session.
- Teacher Directions for Intermediate and Advanced tests are the same.

SCHEDULING AND ADMINISTERING TESTS

1. Administer tests starting in Week 4 of each Thematic Unit while End-of-Unit Assessment is being administered.

2. Teachers can test each group while other students are completing centers, independent work, fluency reading practice, or other reading projects.

3. Administer each section (Vocabulary, Grammar, Reading, and Writing) according to Teacher Directions with Beginning students in one group and Intermediate and Advanced students in another group.

4. In the Writing section, Beginning students should be given only the first page and answer only Test Item 1, while Intermediate and Advanced students should complete both pages.

Skill Level	Approximate Assesment Times			
	Vocabulary	Grammar	Reading	Writing
Beginning	5 minutes	5 minutes	15 minutes	10 minutes
Intermediate/Advanced	5 minutes	5 minutes	20 minutes	15 minutes

Student Self-Assessment

The Student Self-Assessment form provided with each Unit Progress Test allows students to document self-reflection of their own language learning progress and what they have learned from each unit. Students should start working on their Self-Assessment forms the beginning of Week 4.

Beginning English Language Learners
During small group time, guide students through one section per session, allowing additional time for completion during student independent work throughout the week.

Intermediate and Advanced English Language Learners
During small group time, explain one or more sections to students and assign the form to be completed as part of independent work throughout the week.

Numbers 1 through 6 below explain the features of the Self-Assessment form (see the numbered sample Self-Assessment form on page T9).

1 Tell students this form will help them think about what they have learned about reading and speaking in English, and set learning goals.

2 For Beginning English language learners, read and work through each section. Be available to guide Intermediate and Advanced learners when necessary.

3 Encourage students to be honest with their answers. Remind them that this form will not be graded.

4 Explain that "Yes" means students think they really know how to do what the statement says, "Sometimes" means they can do it sometimes, and "Not Yet" means they need help to do it.

5 Have students write the titles of books they have read in English during the unit.

6 Have students write learning goals based on their interests and assessement of what they have learned.

Using the Information

- Review students' Self-Assessment forms to gather additional information about their needs and to note growth in content covered in the unit.

- Review the form to compare students' understanding of their progress with your own understanding of their progress.

- Use the form as a record of progress in parent conferences or student conferences.

- Review students' forms to assess their abilities to respond.

- Photocopy students' forms to include in their portfolios or with their report cards.

- Have students take a copy of the form home to share what they have learned with their families.

- Use the form to provide positive feedback to students on their progress.

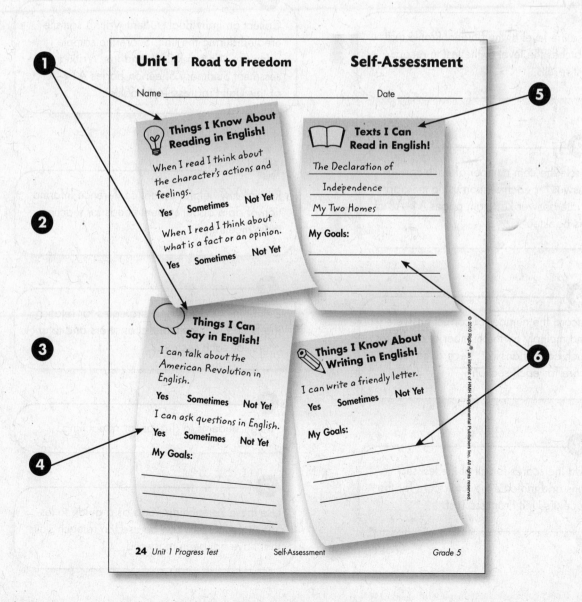

Guiding Instruction

To guide instruction using Unit Progress Tests, teachers need a documentation tool to record and analyze English language learners' progress.

STUDENT PROFILES

The Unit Student Profiles provided with each Unit Progress Test help teachers gather results to identify strengths and weaknesses and to record English language learners' progress in each unit. There are two Student Profiles located after each Unit Progress Test: one for Beginning English language learners and one for Intermediate and Advanced English language learners.

Numbers 1 through 9 below explain the features of the Student Profile (see the numbered sample Student Profile on page T11).

1 Use the level of the Student Profile that matches the level of the test to record test results.

2 Circle the item number of each correct answer for each section using the appropriate answer key from pages A1–A8 of this booklet.

3 Record the number of correct answers and multiply by the number of points for each correct answer. Record the total score for each section.

4 Add the scores for all of the test sections and indicate the total score for the student's Unit Progress Test.

5 Collect an individual student writing sample created during the unit. Score the sample using the Writing Rubric and the Writing Assessment Summary Sheet on pages A14–A16 of this Unit Progress Test booklet.

6 Record any helpful parent conference information or data about student needs for teacher team meetings.

7 Determine the skills and strategies for reteaching based on the incorrect answers and total score for each section.

8 Assign students to groups for reteaching.

9 Use these Reteaching Tools as a guide to lesson materials that can be used to reteach skills that have not been mastered.

Using the information

• Form reteaching groups during small group instruction or centers time.

• Use results to prepare for parent conferences or grade-level meetings to discuss plans to develop students' skills and strategies.

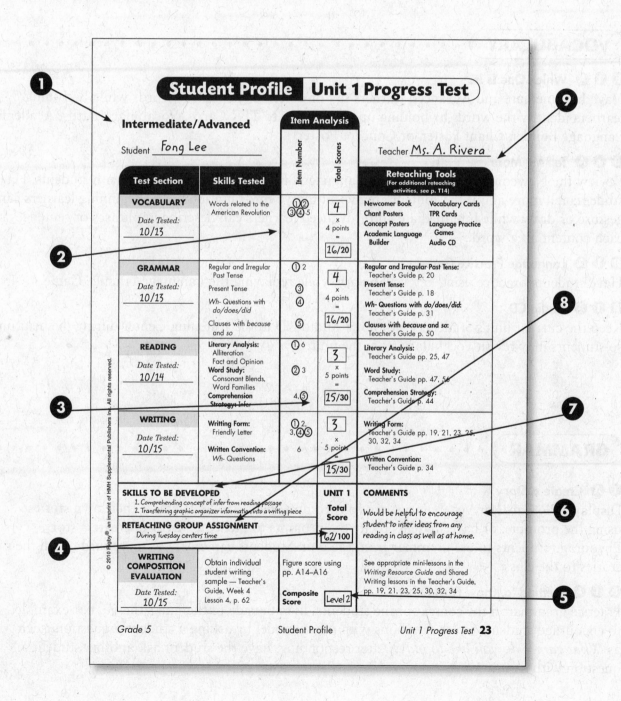

Reteaching Ideas

The Reteaching Tools column on the Student Profile refers teachers to *On Our Way to English* Thematic materials and lessons in order to further develop skills and strategies that do not meet expectations. The following list of activities provides some suggestions for further developing vocabulary, grammar, reading comprehension, and writing process skills using the materials referenced on the Student Profile.

VOCABULARY

Ⓑ Ⓘ Ⓐ Which One Is It?
Have Intermediate and Advanced learners say or describe vocabulary words while Beginning learners identify the words by holding up or pointing to TPR Cards, Vocabulary Cards, Academic Language Builder, Chant Poster, or Concept Poster.

Ⓑ Ⓘ Ⓐ Tell Me More
Review the Newcomer Book, Academic Language Builder, or Concept Poster with students. Have students tell more about the content area vocabulary words in each piece. Beginning learners can gesture or draw while Intermediate and Advanced learners can describe in phrases or sentences each content area word.

Ⓑ Ⓘ Ⓐ Language Practice Game
Have students practice using key vocabulary while replaying the Language Practice Game.

Ⓑ Ⓘ Ⓐ Audio CD
Keep the current unit's Students Anthology Audio CD in the Listening Center during the next unit so students may revisit vocabulary from the unit.

GRAMMAR

Ⓘ Ⓐ Create a Story
Display TPR Cards or Vocabulary Cards as prompts. Have students create their own stories using the prompts, or have students relate the prompts to their own lives to create a story. Encourage students to use grammar from the unit. Students can create a storyboard to tell their stories to the class.

Ⓑ Ⓘ Ⓐ Getting to Know Each Other
Practice grammar in the context of the students' lives outside of the unit's theme. For example, to encourage students to use questions with *what*, model by asking a student a question, such as *What games do you like to play?* After responding, have the student ask another student a question with *what*.

READING ●

Ⓑ ❶ ❶ Reteaching Comprehension Strategies or Literacy Skills

Choose a book students are very familiar with that is a good context in which to teach the strategy or skills. Model the reteaching lesson after the Comprehension Strategy lesson in Week 2 Lesson1 or Literacy Skills lesson in Week 1 Lesson 5 or Week 3 Lesson 2 in each thematic unit of the Thematic Teacher's Guide.

❶ Ⓐ Taking Notes for Reading Comprehension

For nonfiction retelling, use a text that students are familiar with. Model how to take notes on the main idea and details. For main idea, review any headings and read the paragraphs thinking aloud about how to get the main idea of a paragraph. Then reread the paragraphs and think aloud about how to get two important details. Invite students to be the teacher for some paragraphs. Give students opportunities to lead the discussion for each paragraph. Invite students to model how to take notes.

WRITING ●

Ⓑ ❶ Ⓐ Add to the Story

Use Shared Writing Card Side A by covering a picture and its label or adding another space for a picture and its label with a large sticky note. You may choose to cover more than one picture or add more than one space. Elicit other possible pictures or events with labels that would make sense in the blank space or spaces, and proceed with the Shared Writing Card lesson in Week 1 Lesson 3.

❶ Ⓐ Make a Good Paragraph

Use your class writing sample created in Week 1 Lesson 4 with Shared Writing Card Side A. Cut up the paragraph into sentences or rewrite the sentences on sentence strips. Invite students to arrange the sentences into a well-written paragraph. Read, or have students read, the paragraph aloud to see if the paragraph works well as arranged. If needed, invite students to give reasons to rearrange sentences or guide students to understand how the paragraph could be better, allowing them to rearrange the sentences as you discuss.

Student Summary Profiles

The End-of-Year Student Summary Profiles provide teachers with documentation to help measure English language learners' Adequate Yearly Progress through results of the Unit Progress Tests, *Rigby ELL Assessment Kit* reading level assessments, *On Our Way to English* writing composition scores, and *On Our Way to English* Pre- and Post-Retelling assessments. Teachers can see at a glance students' yearly progress of oral language development, reading, and writing.

Numbers 1 through 7 below explain the features of the Student Summary Profile (see numbered sample Student Summary Profile on page T15).

1 Record the level of the student at each Unit Progress Test (Beginning, Intermediate, Advanced).

2 After administering each Unit Progress Test, record the total score of each section from the Student Unit Profile and add up the totals.

3 Record each unit's writing Composite Score from the Student Unit Profiles.

4 Record the reading proficiency level of the student assessed at the beginning, middle, and end of the year using the *Rigby ELL Assessment Kit*

5 Record the student's Unit 1 (beginning-of-year) and Unit 8 (end-of-year) Writing Composition Composite Scores. (See number three.)

6 Record the date and the assessed Stage of Language Acquisition for the Pre-Retelling assessment at the beginning of the year and the Post-Retelling assessment at the end of the year. See the Assessment Handbook.

7 Record any additional observations, such as continued growth or struggles in specific areas.

Using the information

- Use results to prepare for parent conferences.
- Use results to prepare for grade-level meetings to discuss additional plans for the next school year to develop students' skills and strategies.
- Forward this document to the student's next teacher.
- Include as additional documentation for Adequate Yearly Progress.
- Include as district documentation for the next school year.

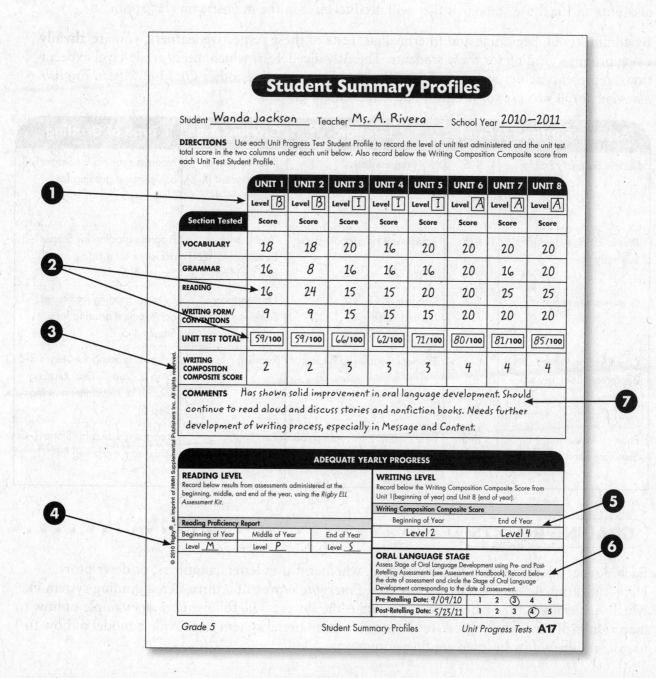

Student Summary Profiles

Student **Wanda Jackson**   Teacher **Ms. A. Rivera**   School Year **2010–2011**

DIRECTIONS Use each Unit Progress Test Student Profile to record the level of unit test administered and the unit test total score in the two columns under each unit below. Also record below the Writing Composition Composite score from each Unit Test Student Profile.

Section Tested	UNIT 1 Level B Score	UNIT 2 Level B Score	UNIT 3 Level I Score	UNIT 4 Level I Score	UNIT 5 Level I Score	UNIT 6 Level A Score	UNIT 7 Level A Score	UNIT 8 Level A Score
VOCABULARY	18	18	20	16	20	20	20	20
GRAMMAR	16	8	16	16	16	20	16	20
READING	16	24	15	15	20	20	25	25
WRITING FORM/CONVENTIONS	9	9	15	15	15	20	20	20
UNIT TEST TOTAL	59/100	59/100	66/100	62/100	71/100	80/100	81/100	85/100
WRITING COMPOSITION COMPOSITE SCORE	2	2	3	3	3	4	4	4

COMMENTS Has shown solid improvement in oral language development. Should continue to read aloud and discuss stories and nonfiction books. Needs further development of writing process, especially in Message and Content.

ADEQUATE YEARLY PROGRESS

READING LEVEL
Record below results from assessments administered at the beginning, middle, and end of the year, using the *Rigby ELL Assessment Kit*.

Reading Proficiency Report

Beginning of Year	Middle of Year	End of Year
Level M	Level P	Level S

WRITING LEVEL
Record below the Writing Composition Composite Score from Unit 1 (beginning of year) and Unit 8 (end of year).

Writing Composition Composite Score

Beginning of Year	End of Year
Level 2	Level 4

ORAL LANGUAGE STAGE
Assess Stage of Oral Language Development using Pre- and Post-Retelling Assessments (see Assessment Handbook). Record below the date of assessment and circle the Stage of Oral Language Development corresponding to the date of assessment.

Pre-Retelling Date: 9/09/10	1	2	③	4	5
Post-Retelling Date: 5/23/11	1	2	3	④	5

Grade 5   Student Summary Profiles   *Unit Progress Tests* **A17**

Assigning Scores and Grading

Two grading systems teachers can use are achievement grading and progress grading. Achievement grading measures students' achievement of a specific task or standard, such as writing using complete sentences. Progress grading measures students' progress toward achievement of a specific task or standard. Progress grading takes into account the progress a student has made from one point in time to another.

In working with English language learners, using progress grading is recommended for Beginning and Intermediate English language learners to take into account students' oral language development in relation to their English literacy. For Advanced English language learners, achievement grading is recommended to challenge them to work toward grade-level standards and hold them accountable for those standards they will need to meet in the mainstream classroom.

By administering Beginning and Intermediate Tests to these respective learners, you are already using progress grading for these students. The Advanced Test, which meets grade-level expectations, represents achievement grading. The chart below outlines other *On Our Way to English* assessment tools to use for progress and achievement grading.

Assessment Tools	Grade	Location	Grading Area	Type of Grading
Student Summary Profile	K–5	Unit Progress Tests booklet, p. A17	Oral Language Development (K–5), Reading and Writing (1–5)	Progress grading for Stages 1–3; achievement grading for Stages 4–5
Thematic Unit Assessment Summary Sheet	K–5	Assessment Handbook, p. 61	Oral Language Development (ESL) and Reading	Progress grading for Stages 1–3; achievement grading for Stages 4–5
Grammar Masters	1–5	Grade-level Skills Masters book	Oral Language Development (ESL)	Progress grading for Stages 1–3; achievement grading for Stages 4–5
Oral Reading Record and Benchmark Book Lessons	K–5	Thematic Teacher's Guide	Reading	Progress grading for Stages 3–5 (Step 6, Step 7, Oral Reading Record); achievement grading (Step 5)
Phonics Assessment Summary Sheet	K–5	Assessment Handbook, p. 68	Reading	Progress grading for Stages 1–3; achievement grading for Stages 4–5

GRADING RESULTS

Each district adopts its own grading system, whether it uses letters, numbers, or descriptors. Here, the terms *Achieving, Developing,* and *Emerging* represent a three-tiered grading system in which *Achieving* is the highest and *Emerging* is the lowest. The following is an example of how to map results of the Unit Progress Tests onto this three-tiered system to provide a model of how to use the results with your own grading system.

Oral Language Grading

Total the scores for both the Vocabulary and Grammar sections of all Unit Progress Tests taken during the grading period (see circles below).

Reading and Writing Grading

Total scores for all Reading sections and for all Writing sections during the grading period (see squares below).

Determine the percentage of correct answers. Use the guidelines below to assign a grade.

80–100%.............Achieving
50–79%...............Developing
Less than 50%.......Emerging

Oral Language Grading Example: If Units 1 and 2 fall within your grading period, the total for Unit 1 Vocabulary and Grammar and Unit 2 Vocabulary and Grammar is 68 (out of a possible 80 points—see student profiles for total possible points), or 85%. You can now assign a score of 85% for that grading period. The student would be *Achieving*, the highest grade in this three-tiered system.

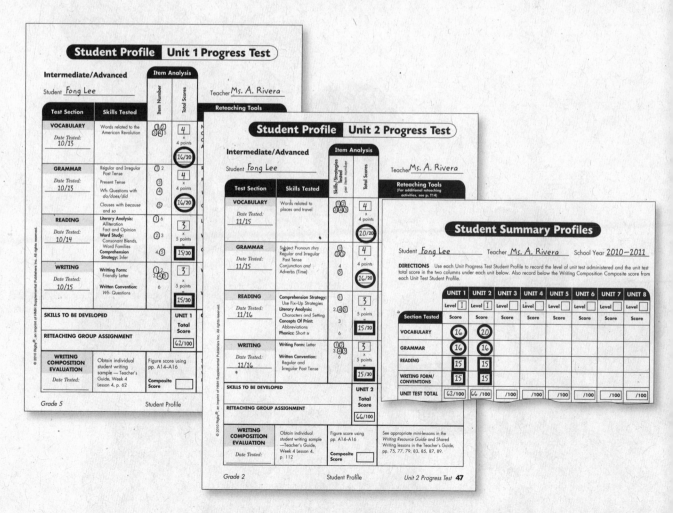

Assessment Throughout the Year

The Yearly Assessment Calendar on page T19 outlines how the *On Our Way to English* Unit Progress Tests fit into the scope of other *On Our Way to English* assessments to conduct during the school year. It is organized in chronological order for convenient reference throughout the school year.

Note in the Yearly Assessment Calendar that the *On Our Way to English* Unit Progress Tests should be administered once a month at the end of each *On Our Way to English* Thematic Unit.

Using the assessments outlined in the Yearly Assessment Calendar throughout the school year allows you to gauge your English language learners' progress and inform your instruction, maximizing students' yearly progress!

Grade 5

On Our Way to English

Unit Progress Tests

On Our Way to English Yearly Assessment Calendar

Assessment Tool	Grades	Location	Area(s) Assessed: *Oral Language Development*	*Literacy*	*Content*	Beginning of the Year	Throughout the Year	End of the Year
Pre- and Post-Retelling; Oral Language Rubric	K–5	Teacher's Guide: pp. A41–42; Assessment Handbook: p.35	•			First two weeks		Last month of school
Reading Checklists	K–5	Assessment Handbook pp. 39, 41, 43, 45		•		First two weeks	Once each grading period	Last month of school
Reading Strategy Checklists	K–5	Assessment Handbook: pp. 40, 42, 44, 46		•		First two weeks	Weekly in guided reading sessions	Last month of school
Oral Reading Record	K–5	Assessment Handbook: p.55	•	•		First month	Every 4–6 weeks	Last month of school
Language and Literacy Profile	K–5	Assessment Handbook: p. 60	•	•		First month	About once a month	Last month of school
Comprehension Assessment Checklists	K–5	Assessment Handbook: p.38		•		First month	Every 4–6 weeks	Last month of school
Letter Recognition and Formation Records	K–1 and newcomers in 2–5	Assessment Handbook: pp. 62–63		•		First month	Every 4–6 weeks, only as needed	Last month as needed
Diagnostic Assessment and Progress Tests on the Interactive Phonics CD-ROM	2–5 as needed	Interactive Phonics CD-ROM		•		First month or as new students enter	As each section is completed	
Writing Evaluation Form; Writing Rubric; Writing Assessment Summary Sheet	K–5	Assessment Handbook: pp. 64–67		•		First month	Once a month with each Thematic Unit	With Thematic Unit 8
Writing Self-assessments	2–5	Writing Resource Guide		•		First month	Month 4	Last month of school
Unit Progress Tests	K–5	**Unit Progress Tests booklet**	•	•	•		Once a month with each Thematic Unit	With Thematic Unit 8
Unit Assessment; Thematic Unit Assessment Summary Sheet	K–5	Teacher's Guide; Assessment Handbook: p. 61	•	•	•		Once a month with each Thematic Unit	With Thematic Unit 8
Open-ended Oral Language Assessment; Oral Language Rubric	K–5	**Unit Progress Tests appendix**; Assessment Handbook: p. 35	•		•		Once a month, at end of each Thematic Unit	With Thematic Unit 8
Language Learning Masters	1–5	Skills Masters book	•	•	•		Throughout the Thematic Units	With Thematic Unit 8
Reading Fluency Assessment	K–5 (stages 4 and 5 only)	Assessment Handbook: p. 47–48	•	•			Every 4–6 weeks with each Benchmark Book	Last month of school
Phonics Assessment Summary Sheet	K–5	Assessment Handbook: p. 68	•				Each week	Last week of school
Standardized Test-Taking Practice	2–5	Standardized Test Practice Masters book		•	•		In early spring, before standardized testing	

Unit 1
Progress Test

Teacher Directions

Road to Freedom

Beginning p. 6

Remind students that this is a test. Tell them that they will complete one test item at a time and that you will read directions for the question.

Sample

Distribute the test pages. Point to the sample box. Tell students to look at the pictures in the box as you say and point to each picture: *This picture shows a* bike. *This picture shows a car. This picture shows a bus. This picture shows a truck.* Ask *Which picture shows a* truck? Wait for students to respond orally. Say *Bubble D is filled in because we were looking for a* truck.

Test Items

Say the following directions for each test item. Then wait for students to bubble in their choice. Tell students to look at you when they finish each item.

1. Have students point to item number 1 and say *Look at the pictures in row one. Which picture shows a* battle? Tell students to bubble in the circle under the picture that shows a *battle.*

2. Have students point to item number 2 and say *Look at the pictures in row two. Which picture shows a person* protesting *something?* Tell students to bubble in the circle under the picture that shows a person *protesting* something.

3. Have students point to item number 3 and say *Look at the pictures in row three. Which picture shows the* Boston Tea Party? Tell students to bubble in the circle under the picture that shows the *Boston Tea Party.*

Intermediate p. 10   Advanced p. 14

Remind students that this is a test. Tell them that they will complete one test item at a time and that you will read directions for the question.

Sample

Distribute the test pages. Point to the sample sentences in the box. Tell students that one word is missing in the sentence. Say *Read these sentences with me. What time is it? I will check the* blank. Say *Now we will read the sentences again with each choice to see which one best*

fits in the blank. *What time is it? I will check the* chair. *I will check the* clock. *I will check the* table. *I will check the* mirror. Ask *Which word would make sense to put in the blank?* Wait for students to respond orally. Tell students that bubble B is filled in because *I will check the clock* is the correct choice.

Test Items

Use the following directions for each test item. Then wait for students to bubble in their choice. Tell students to look at you when they finish each item.

1. Say *Point to test item 1. Read the sentence with me. At the* blank, *some colonists dumped boxes into the water.*
   Then say *Read the sentence again and try each word in the blank.*
   Wait for students to read, then say *Bubble in the choice for the word that goes in the blank.*

2. Say *Point to test item 2. Read the sentence with me. Pennsylvania was a British* blank *before it was a state.*
   Then say *Read the sentence again and try each word in the blank.*
   Wait for students to read, then say *Bubble in the choice for the word that goes in the blank.*

3. Say *Point to test item 3. Read the sentence with me The colonist* blank *the government of King George.*
   Then say *Read the sentence again and try each word in the blank.*
   Wait for students to read, then say *Bubble in the choice for the word that goes in the blank.*

4. Say *Point to test item 4. Read the sentence with me. A* blank *in Lexington between British and American forces helped start the Revolutionary War.*
   Then say *Read the sentence again and try each word in the blank.*
   Wait for students to read, then say *Bubble in the choice for the word that goes in the* blank.

5. Say *Point to test item 5. Read the sentence with me. The soldiers fight for* blank.
   Then say *Read the sentence again and try each word in the blank.*
   Wait for students to read, then say *Bubble in the choice for the word that goes in the blank.*

Teacher Directions

Grammar

Unit 1 Progress Test

Road to Freedom

Beginning p. 7

Remind students that this is a test. Tell them that they will complete one test item at a time and that you will read directions for each question.

Sample

Distribute the test pages. Point to the sample box. Tell students to look at the pictures in the box as you say and point to each picture: *This picture shows a girl eating lunch. This picture shows a girl throwing away her trash after she eats lunch.* Ask *Which picture shows* Moira eats lunch? Wait for students to respond orally. Say *Bubble* A *is filled in because we were looking for the picture that shows* Moira eats lunch.

Test Items

Say the following directions for each test item. Then wait for students to bubble in their choice. Tell students to look at you when they finish each item.

1. Have students point to item number 1 and say *Look at the pictures. Which picture shows* The soldier stands? Tell students to bubble in the choice under the picture that shows *The soldier stands.*

2. Have students point to item number 2 and say *Look at the pictures. Which picture shows* Gloria and Arturo play in the snow? Tell students to bubble in the choice under the picture that shows *Gloria and Arturo play in the snow.*

3. Have students point to item number 3 and say *Look at the pictures. Which picture answers* Where did the dog walk? Tell students to bubble in the choice under the picture that answers *Where did the dog walk?*

4. Have students point to item number 4 and say *Look at the pictures. Which picture answers* Why does Mahala buy lemons? Tell students to bubble in the choice under the picture that answers *Why does Mahala buy lemons?*

 Intermediate p. 11   **Advanced** p. 15

Remind students that this is a test. Tell them that they will complete one test item at a time and that you will read directions for each question.

Sample

Distribute the test pages. Point to the sample sentence in the box. Tell students that one word is missing in the sentence. Say *Read this sentence with me. Yesterday, Jinwon* blank *to some good music.* Say *Now we will read the sentence again with each choice to see which one best fits in the blank. Yesterday, Jinwon* listen *to some good music. Yesterday, Jinwon* listens *to some good music. Yesterday, Jinwon* listened *to some good music. Yesterday, Jinwon* listening *to some good music.* Ask *Which word would make sense to put in the blank?* Wait for students to respond orally. Tell students that bubble C is filled in because *Yesterday, Jinwon* listened *to some good music* is the correct choice.

Test Items

Say the following directions for each test item. Then wait for students to bubble in their choice. Tell students to look at you when they are finished with each item.

1. Say *Point to test item 1. Read the sentence with me. Yesterday, Mrs. Cheng* blank *our lunch at school.* Then say *Read the sentence and try each answer choice in the blank.* Wait for students to read. Then say *Bubble in the choice for the answer that goes in the blank.*

2. Say *Point to test item 2. Read the sentence with me. The students* blank *their cans in the box.* Then say *Read the sentence and try each answer choice in the blank.* Wait for students to read. Then say *Bubble in the choice for the answer that goes in the blank.*

3. Say *Point to test item 3. Read the sentence with me. Donovan* blank *a baseball so he can play.* Then say *Read the sentence and try each answer choice in the blank.* Wait for students to read. Then say *Bubble in the choice for the answer that goes in the blank.*

4. Say *Point to test item 4. Read the sentence with me.* Blank *did Emily break her leg?* Then say *Read the sentence and try each answer choice in the blank.* Wait for students to read. Then say *Bubble in the choice for the answer that goes in the blank.*

5. Say *Point to test item 5. Read the sentence with me. Kelvin is happy* blank *his mom gave him an apple.* Then say *Read the sentence and try each answer choice in the blank.* Wait for students to read. Then say *Bubble in the choice for the answer that goes in the blank.*

Beginning pp. 8–9

Remind students that this is a test. Tell them that they will complete one test item at a time and that you will read directions for each question.

Passage

Distribute test page 8. Have students point to the pictures in the box. Explain that Sybil Ludington was a teenage girl who helped her town during the Revolutionary War. Tell students that you will read the passage aloud to them before moving on to the test items. Because this passage is a play, you may want to vary your voice to indicate changes in speakers. Invite students to listen as you read the passage aloud.

Say *Listen as I read the story, "Sybil's Ride."*

1. *Look at Picture 1:* **Sybil:** *Father, I think you're a brave soldier.*

   Father: *I'm proud to fight for freedom!*

2. *Look at Picture 2:* **Narrator:** *There's a knock at the door.*

   Messenger: *Colonel, the British are burning the next town!*

   Father: *Warn everyone—quickly!*

   Messenger: *I feel too tired for the trip.*

3. *Look at Picture 3:* **Sybil:** *I'll go! I could help the colonies!*

4. *Look at Picture 4:* **Narrator:** *Sybil rode all night. She helped the colonists win independence.*

Test Items

Distribute test page 9. Use the following directions for each test item. Read aloud the question. Give students time to read and look at the pictures. Then wait for students to bubble in their choice. Tell students to look at you when they finish each item.

1. Say *Point to test item 1. Listen to this sentence from the story: I feel too tired for the* **trip.** *Look at the words. Listen to the question and choices with me. Which word shows* trip: trip, try, trade, tree? *Bubble in the choice that shows the word* **trip.**

2. Say *Point to test item 2. Which sentence from the story is a fact? Read each sentence and look at each picture.* Say *Bubble in the choice that tells a fact.*

3. Say *Point to test item 3. What can you tell about Sybil from the story? Read each sentence and look at each picture. Bubble in the choice that answers the question What can you tell about Sybil from the story?*

4. Say *Point to test item 4. How does Sybil help the colonists? Read each sentence and look at each picture. Bubble in the choice that answers the question How does Sybil help the colonists?*

Intermediate pp. 12–13   **Advanced** pp. 16–18

Remind students that this is a test. Explain that they will read the passage on their own and complete the test items.

Passage

Distribute the reading passages. Tell students that they are going to read about a brave teenage girl named Sybil Ludington who protected her town during the Revolutionary War. Ask students to read the passage independently and to look at you when they have finished.

Test Items

Distribute the test pages. Remind students that they may look back at the passage for help in answering questions.

1. Say *Point to test item 1. Which of these words from the story is an example of alliteration?* Wait for students to bubble in their choice. Tell students to look at you when they are finished.

2. Say *Point to test item 2. Listen to this sentence from the story: I feel too tired for the* **trip.** *Look at the words. Listen to the question and choices with me. Which word has the* **tr-** *sound like* **trip:** trap, tap, flap, slip? *Bubble in the choice that has the* **tr-** *sound like* **trip.**

3. Say *Point to test item 3. Listen to this sentence from the story: I can do* **that.** *Look at the words. Listen to the question and choices with me. Which word has the* **-at** *sound like* **that:** they, clot, flat, tail. *Bubble in the choice for the word that has the* **-at** *sound like* **that.**

   Tell students that they will complete the rest of the test by themselves.

Teacher Directions

Writing

Beginning p. 20

Remind students that this is a test. Tell them that they will complete one test item and that you will read directions for each question. Point to the graphic organizer. Explain to students that Peng, a fifth grade student, filled in a graphic organizer about her class trip to Yorktown before writing a friendly letter to her grandmother.

Test Item 1

Point to the Greeting and Topic space. Say *Peng wants to write to her grandmother about her visit to Yorktown, Virginia.* Say *Look at the pictures and the things she wrote about this trip. Peng wrote "Rode to Yorktown," "Visit to the Yorktown Victory Center" and "Visit to the war camp."* Point to the missing picture in box 1. Say *Peng is also going to talk about how her trip to Yorktown started.* Point to test item 1 and say *Bubble in the choice for the picture that best fits in box 1.* Wait for students to bubble their choice. Tell students to look at you when they are finished.

Intermediate/Advanced pp. 20–21

Remind students that this is a test. Tell them that they will complete one test item at a time and that you will read directions for each question. Point to the graphic organizer. Explain to students that Peng, a fifth grade student, filled in a graphic organizer about her class trip to Yorktown, Virginia, before writing a friendly letter to her grandmother. Tell them that they will want to use Peng's graphic organizer and her letter on page 21 to answer questions on both pages.

Test Item 1

Point to the missing picture in box 1 and say *There is a picture missing. Read what Peng wrote about her visit to Yorktown and look at the pictures.* Wait for students to read the graphic organizer and letter. Point to test item 1 and say *Bubble in the choice for the picture that best fits in box 1.* Wait for students to bubble their choice. Tell students to look at you when they are finished.

Test Item 2

Point to the blank line (2) under the closing and say *Write the word that Peng forgot to write.* Wait for students to write the closing on the blank line. Tell students to look at you when they are finished.

Tell students that they are going to read what Peng wrote after filling in the graphic organizer on page 20. Tell students that they can go back to the graphic organizer and see what Peng wrote first. Point to the missing sentences in the writing sample, and say *There are two sentences missing.* Tell students *Read to see what is missing.* Wait for students to read the writing sample. Tell students to look at you when they are finished. Remind students to use both the graphic torganizer and the paragraph to answer test items 3, 4 and 5.

Test Item 3

Point to test item 3 and say *Read the question and bubble in the choice for blank three.* Wait for students to mark their answers. Tell students to look at you when they are finished.

Test Item 4

Point to test item 4 and say *Read the question and bubble in the choice for blank four.* Wait for students to mark their answers. Tell students to look at you when they are finished.

Test Item 5

Point to test item 5 and say. *Read the question and bubble in your answer choice.* Wait for students to mark their answers. Tell students to look at you when they are finished.

Test Item 6

Point to the sentences in the box at the bottom of the page. Say *Peng's friend, Alberto, wrote these sentences about the class trip to Yorktown.* Tell students *One of Alberto's sentences has a mistake.* Ask students to help Alberto fix his sentence. Say *Find the mistake in the first sentence and bubble in the choice for the sentence that would correct it.* Wait for students to mark their answer. Tell students to look at you when they are finished.

Unit 1 Road to Freedom

Vocabulary Ⓑ

Name _____ Date _____

Directions Look at the pictures. Listen to the question.
Bubble in the circle underneath the picture for your answer.

Sample

Ⓐ   Ⓑ   Ⓒ   Ⓓ

1

Ⓐ   Ⓑ   Ⓒ   Ⓓ

2

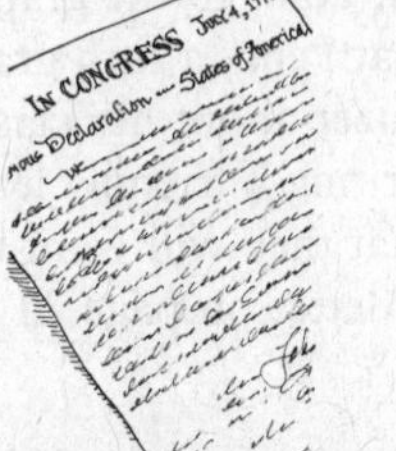

Ⓐ   Ⓑ   Ⓒ   Ⓓ

3

Ⓐ   Ⓑ   Ⓒ   Ⓓ

Unit 1 Road to Freedom

Grammar Ⓑ

Name _____ Date _____

Directions Look at the pictures. Listen to the question. Bubble in the circle underneath the picture for your answer.

Sample

TRAYS

Ⓐ   Ⓑ

1

Ⓐ   Ⓑ

3

Ⓐ   Ⓑ

2

Ⓐ   Ⓑ

4

Lemons 4/$1.00 Apples $1.39

Lemonade 10¢

Ⓐ   Ⓑ

Unit 1 Road to Freedom

Name _____ Date _____

Directions Listen to the selection. Then listen to each question. Choose the best answer. Bubble in your answer.

CHARACTERS
Narrator
Sybil Ludington
Sybil's father,
   Colonel Ludington
Messenger

Sybil's Ride

1 *Sybil:* Father, I think you're a
   brave soldier.

   Father: I'm proud to fight for
   freedom!

2 *Narrator:* There's a knock at
   the door.

   Messenger: Colonel, the British are
   burning the next town!

   Father: Warn everyone—
   quickly!

   Messenger:
   I feel too tired
   for the trip.

3 *Sybil:* I'll go! I could help
   the colonies!

4 *Narrator:* Sybil rode all night. She
   helped the colonists win
   independence.

Name _____ Date _____

1

trip	try	trade	tree
Ⓔ	Ⓕ	Ⓖ	Ⓗ

2 Which sentence from the story is a fact?

I could help
the colonies!

Ⓐ

I feel too tired
for the trip.

Ⓑ

I'm proud to fight
for freedom!

Ⓒ

Sybil rode
all night.

Ⓓ

3 What can you tell about Sybil from the story?

Sybil loves horses.

Ⓐ

Sybil is British.

Ⓑ

Sybil is married to
the Messenger.

Ⓒ

Sybil wants to be
part of the fight
for freedom.

Ⓓ

4 How does Sybil help the colonists?

She gives a horse
to every soldier.

Ⓐ

She tells the
British about her
brave father.

Ⓑ

She warns the
colonists about the
British.

Ⓒ

She stays at home.

Ⓓ

Unit 1   Road to Freedom   Vocabulary ❶

Name _____   Date _____

Directions Read the sentence. Choose the word or
words that best fit in the blank. Bubble in your answer.

SAMPLE

What time is it? I will
check the _____.

Ⓐ chair
Ⓑ clock
Ⓒ table
Ⓓ mirror

---

1 At the _____, some
colonists dumped boxes
into the water.
Ⓐ July 4th
Ⓑ colony
Ⓒ Boston Tea Party
Ⓓ Declaration of
Independence

2 Pennsylvania was a
British _____
before it was a state.
Ⓔ King George
Ⓕ colony
Ⓖ freedom
Ⓗ pamphlet

3 The colonist_____
the government of King
George.
Ⓐ declares
Ⓑ refuses
Ⓒ protests
Ⓓ march

4 A _____ in Lexington
between British and
American forces helped
start the Revolutionary
War.
Ⓔ colony
Ⓕ constitution
Ⓖ revolution
Ⓗ battle

5 The soldiers fight for _____.
Ⓐ pamphlet
Ⓑ July 4th
Ⓒ colony
Ⓓ liberty

Name _____   Date _____

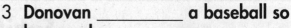

Directions Read the sentence. Choose the word or words that best fit in the blank. Bubble in your answer.

SAMPLE

Yesterday, Jinwon _____ to some good music.

- (A) listen
- (B) listens
- (C) listened
- (D) listening

---

1 Yesterday, Mrs. Cheng _____ our lunch at school.

- (A) cook
- (B) does cook
- (C) cooked
- (D) cooking

---

2 The students _____ their cans in the box.

- (E) threw
- (F) throwing
- (G) does throw
- (H) thrown

---

3 Donovan _____ a baseball so he can play.

- (A) buy
- (B) buying
- (C) buys
- (D) do buy

---

4 _____ did Emily break her leg?

- (E) When
- (F) Who
- (G) When was
- (H) What

---

5 Kelvin is happy _____ his mom gave him an apple.

- (A) yet
- (B) because
- (C) so that
- (D) if

Name _____   Date _____

Directions Read the selection. Then listen to each question. Choose the best answer. Bubble in your answer.

CHARACTERS

Narrator
Sybil Ludington
Sybil's father,
   Colonel Ludington
Messenger

Sybil's Ride

Narrator:	Sybil Ludington lives in New York in 1777.
Sybil:	Father, I think you're a brave soldier.
Father:	I'm proud to fight for freedom!
Narrator:	Suddenly, a messenger arrives.
Messenger:	Colonel, the British are burning the next town!
Father:	Go and warn everyone!
Messenger:	I feel too tired for the trip.
Sybil:	I can do that. I'll go! I could help the colonies!
Narrator:	Sybil rode all night. She protected her town during the Revolutionary War.

Name _____   Date _____

1 Which of these words from the story is an example of alliteration?
- Ⓐ a brave soldier
- Ⓑ too tired for the trip
- Ⓒ a messenger arrives
- Ⓓ the Revolutionary War

2
- Ⓔ trap
- Ⓕ tap
- Ⓖ flap
- Ⓗ slip

3
- Ⓐ they
- Ⓑ clot
- Ⓒ flat
- Ⓓ tail

4 What can you tell about Sybil Ludington from the story?
- Ⓔ She is British.
- Ⓕ She wants to be part of the fight for freedom.
- Ⓖ She loves her horse.
- Ⓗ She is married to the Messenger.

5 How did Sybil protect her town?
- Ⓐ She told the British about her brave father.
- Ⓑ She gave a horse to every soldier.
- Ⓒ She warned the colonists about the British attack.
- Ⓓ She told the colonists the Messenger is tired.

6 Which of these sentences from the story is an opinion?
- Ⓔ Sybil Ludington lives in New York in 1777.
- Ⓕ Father, I think you're a brave soldier.
- Ⓖ She protected her town during the Revolutionary War.
- Ⓗ Colonel, the British are burning the next town!

Name _____ Date _____

Directions Read the sentence. Choose the word or words that best fit in the blank. Bubble in your answer.

SAMPLE

What time is it? I will check the _____.
- Ⓐ chair
- Ⓑ clock
- Ⓒ table
- Ⓓ mirror

---

1 At the _____, some colonists dumped boxes into the water.
- Ⓐ July 4th
- Ⓑ colony
- Ⓒ Boston Tea Party
- Ⓓ Declaration of Independence

2 Pennsylvania was a British _____ before it was a state.
- Ⓔ King George
- Ⓕ colony
- Ⓖ freedom
- Ⓗ pamphlet

3 The colonist _____ the government of King George.
- Ⓐ declares
- Ⓑ refuses
- Ⓒ protests
- Ⓓ march

4 A _____ in Lexington between British and American forces helped start the Revolutionary War.
- Ⓔ colony
- Ⓕ constitution
- Ⓖ revolution
- Ⓗ battle

5 The soldiers fight for _____.
- Ⓐ pamphlet
- Ⓑ July 4th
- Ⓒ colony
- Ⓓ liberty

Unit 1 Road to Freedom

Grammar Ⓐ

Name _____ Date _____

Directions Read the sentence. Choose the word or words that best fit in the blank. Bubble in your answer.

SAMPLE

Yesterday, Jinwon _____ to some good music.
- Ⓐ listen
- Ⓑ listens
- Ⓒ listened
- Ⓓ listening

---

1 Yesterday, Mrs. Cheng _____ our lunch at school.
- Ⓐ cook
- Ⓑ does cook
- Ⓒ cooked
- Ⓓ cooking

2 The students _____ their cans in the box.
- Ⓔ threw
- Ⓕ throwing
- Ⓖ does throw
- Ⓗ thrown

3 Donovan _____ a baseball so he can play.
- Ⓐ buy
- Ⓑ buying
- Ⓒ buys
- Ⓓ do buy

4 _____ did Emily break her leg?
- Ⓔ When
- Ⓕ Who
- Ⓖ When was
- Ⓗ What

5 Kelvin is happy _____ his mom gave him an apple.
- Ⓐ yet
- Ⓑ because
- Ⓒ so that
- Ⓓ if

Directions Read the selection. Then listen to each question. Choose the best answer. Bubble in your answer.

CHARACTERS

Narrator
Sybil Ludington
Sybil's father,
  Colonel Ludington
Messenger

Sybil's Ride

Narrator:	It is 1777, during the Revolutionary War. Sybil Ludington lives in New York.
Sybil:	Father, what is it like to lead a group of soldiers?
Father:	Fighting the British army is difficult. But I believe we'll have a better life once we are free!
Narrator:	Suddenly, a messenger arrives.
Messenger:	Colonel, the British are attacking just 15 miles away, where our weapons are stored.

Name _____   Date _____

Father:	Ride through the night and tell everyone!
Messenger:	I feel too tired for the trip.
Sybil:	I'll go, Father. I can do that. I want to be a part of our fight for independence.
Narrator:	Sybil rode her horse all through the night. She warned the colonists of the danger. She helped to protect her town during the colonies' fight for freedom.

Unit 1 Road to Freedom

Reading (A)

Name _____ Date _____

1 **Which of these words from the story is an example of alliteration?**
Ⓐ a brave soldier
Ⓑ too tired for the trip
Ⓒ a messenger arrives
Ⓓ the Revolutionary War

2
Ⓔ trap
Ⓕ tap
Ⓖ flap
Ⓗ slip

3
Ⓐ they
Ⓑ clot
Ⓒ flat
Ⓓ tail

4 **What can you tell about Sybil Ludington from the story?**
Ⓔ She is British.
Ⓕ She wants to be part of the fight for freedom.
Ⓖ She loves her horse.
Ⓗ She is married to the Messenger.

5 **How did Sybil protect her town?**
Ⓐ She told the British about her brave father.
Ⓑ She gave a horse to every soldier.
Ⓒ She warned the colonists about the British attack.
Ⓓ She told the colonists the Messenger is tired.

6 **Which of these sentences from the story is an opinion?**
Ⓔ Sybil Ludington lives in New York.
Ⓕ I believe we'll have a better life once we are free!
Ⓖ She warned the colonists of the danger.
Ⓗ Father, what is it like to lead a group of soldiers?

© 2010 Rigby®, an imprint of HMH Supplemental Publishers Inc. All rights reserved.

Writing

Directions Look at the following graphic organizer and student sample writing on page 21. Then answer the questions.

Date

> October 19, 2009

Greeting

> Dear Grandma,

Body

Topic	A visit to Yorktown, Virginia
1	Rode to Yorktown
	Visit to the Yorktown Victory Center
	Visit to the war camp

Closing

> 2 _____ Granddaughter,
> Peng

1 **Which picture best fits in box 1?**

2 **Fill in blank 2.**

Ⓐ   Ⓑ

Name _____ Date _____

October 19, 2009

Dear Grandma,

(3) _____. We took a school bus to the Yorktown Victory Center.

(4) _____. After that, we saw a camp where people were dressed as soldiers and tents like during the war. Visiting the Yorktown Visitor Center was very interesting and I learned a lot. I will show you my pictures when you come for a visit.

Your Granddaughter,

. Peng

---

3 Which sentence best fits in blank 3?

Ⓐ The Declaration of Independence was signed on July 4, 1776.

Ⓑ Our class took a field trip to Yorktown, Virginia, where the Revolutionary War ended.

Ⓒ My favorite museum is the science museum, where there are models of the planets.

4 Which sentence best fits in blank 4?

Ⓐ At the Victory Center, we tried on colonial clothes, and we learned about what happened during the war.

Ⓑ I want to take my baseball glove to the museum next time.

Ⓒ My grandmother is interested in the Revolutionary War.

5 What is a different closing that Peng could have written?

Ⓐ Dear Grandmother,

Ⓑ I will show you my pictures when I see you.

Ⓒ Love, Peng

Who were you see at the Revolutionary War museum? When do we visit Yorktown together?

---

6 What would make the first sentence in the box above correct?

Ⓐ When do you see at the Revolutionary War museum?

Ⓑ What did you see at the Revolutionary War museum?

Ⓒ What did you see at the Revolutionary War museum.

Student Profile | Unit 1 Progress Test

Beginning

Student _____

Teacher _____

Test Section	Skills Tested	Item Number	Total Scores	Reteaching Tools (For additional reteaching activities, see p. T14)
VOCABULARY Date Tested: _____	Words related to the American Revolution	1, 2, 3	□ × 9 points = /30	**Newcomer Book** **Chant Posters** **Concept Posters** **Academic Language Builder** **Vocabulary Cards** **TPR Cards** **Language Practice Games** **Audio CD**
GRAMMAR Date Tested: _____	Present Tense *Wh-* Questions with *do/does/did*	1, 2 3, 4	□ × 8 points = /32	**Present Tense:** Teacher's Guide p. 18 ***Wh-* Questions with *do/does/did*:** Teacher's Guide p. 31
READING Date Tested: _____	**Word Study:** Consonant Blends **Literary Analysis:** Fact and Opinion **Comprehension Strategy:** Infer	1 2 3, 4	□ × 8 points = /32	**Word Study:** Teacher's Guide p. 47 **Literary Analysis:** Teacher's Guide p. 35 **Comprehension Strategy:** Teacher's Guide p. 44
WRITING Date Tested: _____	**Writing Form:** Friendly Letter	1	□ × 9 points = /9	**Writing Form:** Teacher's Guide pp. 19, 21, 23, 25, 30, 32, 34
SKILLS TO BE DEVELOPED _____ **RETEACHING GROUP ASSIGNMENT**			**UNIT 1 Total Score** /100	**COMMENTS**
WRITING COMPOSITION EVALUATION Date Tested: _____	Obtain individual student writing sample — Teacher's Guide, Week 4 Lesson 4, p. 62	Figure score using pp. A14–A16 **Composite Score** □		See appropriate mini-lessons in the *Writing Resource Guide* and Shared Writing lessons in the Teacher's Guide, pp. 19, 21, 23, 25, 30, 32, 34

Student Profile | Unit 1 Progress Test

Intermediate/Advanced

Student _____   Teacher _____

Item Analysis

Test Section	Skills Tested	Item Number	Total Scores	Reteaching Tools (For additional reteaching activities, see p. T14)
VOCABULARY Date Tested: _____	Words related to the American Revolution	1, 2, 3, 4, 5	☐ x 4 points = /20	Newcomer Book · Vocabulary Cards Chant Posters · TPR Cards Concept Posters · Language Practice Games Academic Language Builder · Audio CD
GRAMMAR Date Tested: _____	Regular and Irregular Past Tense Present Tense Wh- Questions with do/does/did Clauses with because and so	1, 2 3 4 5	☐ x 4 points = /20	**Regular and Irregular Past Tense:** Teacher's Guide p. 20 **Present Tense:** Teacher's Guide p. 18 **Wh- Questions with do/does/did:** Teacher's Guide p. 31 **Clauses with because and so:** Teacher's Guide p. 50
READING Date Tested: _____	**Literary Analysis:** Alliteration Fact and Opinion **Word Study:** Consonant Blends, Word Families **Comprehension Strategy:** Infer	1, 6 2, 3 4, 5	☐ x 5 points = /30	**Literary Analysis:** Teacher's Guide pp. 25, 47 **Word Study:** Teacher's Guide pp. 47, 56 **Comprehension Strategy:** Teacher's Guide p. 44
WRITING Date Tested: _____	**Writting Form:** Friendly Letter **Written Convention:** Wh- Questions	1, 2, 3, 4, 5 6	☐ x 5 points = /30	**Writing Form:** Teacher's Guide pp. 19, 21, 23, 25, 30, 32, 34 **Written Convention:** Teacher's Guide p. 34

SKILLS TO BE DEVELOPED		UNIT 1	COMMENTS
		Total Score	
RETEACHING GROUP ASSIGNMENT		/100	
WRITING COMPOSITION EVALUATION Date Tested: _____	Obtain individual student writing sample — Teacher's Guide, Week 4 Lesson 4, p. 62	Figure score using pp. A14–A16 **Composite Score** ☐	See appropriate mini-lessons in the *Writing Resource Guide* and Shared Writing lessons in the Teacher's Guide, pp. 19, 21, 23, 25, 30, 32, 34

Unit 1 Road to Freedom

Self-Assessment

Name _____ Date _____

Things I Know About Reading in English!

When I read I think about the character's actions and feelings.

Yes   Sometimes   Not Yet

When I read I think about what is a fact or an opinion.

Yes   Sometimes   Not Yet

Texts I Can Read in English!

The Declaration of
_____

Independence
_____

My Two Homes
_____

My Goals:

_____

_____

_____

Things I Can Say in English!

I can talk about the American Revolution in English.

Yes   Sometimes   Not Yet

I can ask questions in English.

Yes   Sometimes   Not Yet

My Goals:

_____

_____

_____

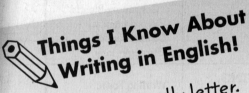

Things I Know About Writing in English!

I can write a friendly letter.

Yes   Sometimes   Not Yet

My Goals:

_____

_____

Unit 2
Progress Test

Beginning p. 30

Remind students that this is a test. Tell them that they will complete one test item at a time and that you will read directions for the questions.

Sample

Distribute the test page. Point to the sample box. Tell students to look at the pictures in the box as you say and point to each picture: *This picture shows* the Boston Tea Party. *This picture shows* a battle. *This picture shows* the Declaration of Independence. *This picture shows* freedom. Ask *Which picture shows* the Declaration of Independence? Wait for students to respond orally. Say *Bubble C is filled in because we were looking for the* Declaration of Independence.

Test Items

Use the following directions for each test item. Wait for students to bubble in their choice. Tell students to look at you when they are finished with each item.

1. Have students point to item number 1 and say *Look at the pictures in row one. Which picture shows a* political party?

   Tell students to bubble in the circle under the picture that shows a *political party.*

2. Have students point to item number 2 and say *Look at the pictures in row two. Which picture shows the* Supreme Court?

   Tell students to bubble in the circle under the picture that shows the *Supreme Court.*

3. Have students point to item number 3 and say *Look at the pictures in row three. Which picture shows a person in the* executive branch?

   Tell students to bubble in the circle under the picture that shows a person in the *executive branch.*

Intermediate p. 34   Advanced p. 38

Remind students that this is a test. Tell them that they will complete one test item at a time and that you will read directions for each question.

Sample

Distribute the test pages. Point to the sample sentence in the box. Tell students that one word is missing in the sentence. Say *Read this sentence with me. People from each* blank *helped win the war.* Say *Now we will read the sentence again with each choice to see which one best fits in the blank. People from each* tax *helped win the war. People from each* colony *helped win the war. People from each* freedom *helped win the war. People from each* pamphlet *helped win the war.* Ask *Which word would make sense to put in the blank?* Wait for students to respond orally. Tell students that bubble *B* is filled in because *People from each colony helped win the war* is the correct choice.

Test Items

Say the following directions for each test item, then wait for students to bubble in their choice. Tell students to look at you when they are finished with each item.

1. Say *Point to test item 1. Read the sentence with me. The legislative branch has* blank. Then say *Read the sentence again and try each word in the blank.* Wait for students to read, then say *Bubble in the choice for the word that goes in the blank.*

2. Say *Point to test item 2. Read the sentence with me. The President is the head of the* blank. Then say *Read the sentence again and try each word in the blank.* Wait for students to read, then say *Bubble in the choice for the word that goes in the blank.*

3. Say *Point to test item 3. Read the sentence with me. United States citizens have* blank *because of the Constitution.* Then say *Read the sentence again and try each word in the blank.* Wait for students to read, then say *Bubble in the choice for the word that goes in the blank.*

4. Say *Point to test item 4. Read the sentence with me. A group of people with the same ideas about government is a* blank. Then say *Read the sentence again and try each word in the blank.* Wait for students to read, then say *Bubble in the choice for the word that goes in the blank.*

5. Say *Point to test item 5. Read the sentence with me. The judicial branch has the* blank. Then say *Read the sentence again and try each word in the blank.* Wait for students to read, then say *Bubble in the choice for the word that goes in the blank.*

Teacher Directions | Unit 2 Progress Test

By the People

Beginning p. 31

Remind students that this is a test. Tell them that they will complete one test item at a time and that you will read directions for each question.

Sample

Distribute the test page. Point to the sample box. Tell students to look at the pictures in the box as you say and point to each picture: *This picture shows a girl buying lemons. This picture shows a girl selling lemonade. Which picture shows* Why does Mahala buy lemons? Wait for students to respond orally. Say *Bubble B is filled in because we were looking for the picture that shows* Why does Mahala buy lemons?

Test Items

Use the following directions for each test item. Then wait for students to bubble in their choice. Tell students to look at you when they are finished with each item.

1. Have students point to item number 1 and say *Look at the pictures. Which picture shows* He has a new bike?

   Tell students to bubble in the circle under the picture that shows *He has a new bike.*

2. Have students point to item number 2 and say *Look at the pictures. Which of these two nouns shows a thing?*

   Tell students to bubble in the circle under the picture that shows a thing.

3. Have students point to item number 3 and say *Look at the pictures. Which picture shows* They have lunch.

   Tell students to bubble in the circle under the picture that shows *They have lunch.*

4. Have students point to item number 4 and say *Look at the pictures. Which of these two nouns shows a place?*

   Tell students to bubble in the circle under the picture that shows a place.

Intermediate p. 35   Advanced p. 39

Remind students that this is a test. Tell them that they will complete one test item at a time and that you will read directions for each question.

Sample

Distribute the test pages. Point to the sample sentence in the box. Tell students that one word is missing in the sentence. Say *Read this sentence with me.* Where blank *Mr. Ting going?* Say *Now we will read the sentence again with each choice to see which one best fits in the blank.* Where was *Mr. Ting going?* Where do *Mr. Ting going?* Where have *Mr. Ting going?* Where does *Mr. Ting going?* Ask *Which answer would make sense to put in the blank?* Wait for students to respond orally. Tell students that bubble A is filled in because *Where was Mr. Ting going?* is the correct choice.

Test Items

Use the following directions for each test item. Then wait for students to bubble in their choice. Tell students to look at you when they are finished with each item.

1. Say *Point to test item 1. Read the sentence with me. Susita likes pink shells,* blank *Marco likes white shells.* Then say *Read the sentence again and try each word in the blank.*

   Wait for students to read, then say *Bubble in the choice for the word that goes in the blank.*

2. Say *Point to test item 2. Read the sentence with me. The book that Pedro reads is* blank. Then say *Read the sentence again and try each word in the blank.*

   Wait for students to read, then say *Bubble in the choice for the word that goes in the blank.*

3. Say *Point to test item 3. Read the sentence with me. Monique has the right* blank *safe.* Then say *Read the sentence again and try each word in the blank.*

   Wait for students to read, then say *Bubble in the choice for the word that goes in the blank.*

4. Say *Point to test item 4. Read the sentence with me. Blank horse jumps high.* Then say *Read the sentence again and try each word in the blank.*

   Wait for students to read, then say *Bubble in the choice for the word that goes in the blank.*

5. Say *Point to test item 5. Read the sentence with me. The canoe* blank *quiet on the water.* Then say *Read the sentence again and try each word in the blank.*

   Wait for students to read, then say *Bubble in the choice for the word that goes in the blank.*

Teacher Directions | Unit 2 Progress Test

By the People

Remind students that this is a test. Tell them that they will complete one test item at a time and that you will read directions for each question.

Passage

Distribute test page 32. Have students point to the pictures in the boxes. Explain that this passage is about the branches of the government and the buildings where each branch works. Ask students to follow along as you read the passage aloud. Point to each illustration as you read the corresponding text.

Say *Listen as I read the story* "Government Branches and Buildings."

1. *Look at picture 1.*   *The U.S. government has three branches.*
Each branch has a different building.

2. *Look at picture 2.*   *Congress is the Legislative Branch. Congress works in the Capitol.*
Congress votes on new laws called bills. Congress sends the bills to the Executive Branch.

3. *Look at picture 3.*   *The Executive Branch works in the White House.*
The President is the head of this branch.

4. *Look at picture 4.*   *The Judicial Branch works in the Supreme Court building.*
The Supreme Court Justices decide what the laws mean.

Test Items

Distribute test page 33. Use the following directions for each test item. Read aloud the questions. Give students time to read and look at the pictures. Then wait for students to bubble in their choice. Tell students to look at you when they are finished with each item.

1. Say *Point to test item 1. Look at the pictures. Read the question with me. Where does the Legislative Branch work? Bubble in the choice that tells where the Legislative Branch works.*

2. Say *Point to test item 2. Look at the pictures. Read the question with me. Which picture answers the question* Where does the President work? *Bubble in the choice that answers the question* Where does the President work?

3. Say *Point to test item 3. Look at the pictures. Read the question with me. Which word is a proper noun? Bubble in the choice that shows a proper noun.*

4. Say *Point to test item 4. Look at the pictures. Read the question with me. Where does Congress send bills after it votes? Bubble in the choice that tells where Congress sends bills after it votes.*

Remind students that this is a test.

Passage

Distribute the reading passages. Tell students they are going to read about the branches of our government and the buildings where the branches work. Ask students to read the passage independently and to look at you when they are finished.

Test Items

Distribute the test pages. Remind students that they will look back at the passage for help in answering questions.

Point to the chart in test item 1. Say *This chart shows the government branches and buildings. Read the question with me. Look at the chart. Which word goes in the chart? Read and bubble in the choice that tells what goes in the chart.* Wait for students to bubble in their choice. Tell students to look at you when they are finished.

Tell students that they will complete the rest of the test by themselves.

Beginning p. 44

Remind students that this is a test. Tell them that they will complete one test item and that you will read directions for each question. Point to the graphic organizer. Explain that Felipe, a fifth grade student, filled in this graphic organizer before writing a letter to the President of the United States requesting that sea turtles be protected.

Test Item 1

Point to the Details space and tell students that the pictures support Felipe's request. Say *Felipe planned a letter to the President of the United States asking him to protect the sea turtles.* Point to the two pictures and filled-in details. Say *In his plan, Felipe noted ideas and reasons for protecting the turtles.*

Point to the missing picture in box 1. Say *Felipe wants the President to do something to help the turtles.* Point to test item 1 and say *Bubble in the choice for the picture that shows one way Felipe wants to help the turtles.* Wait for students to bubble in their choice. Tell students to look at you when they are finished.

Intermediate/Advanced pp. 44–45

Remind students that this is a test. Tell them that they will complete one test item at a time and that you will read directions for each question. Point to the graphic organizer. Explain that Felipe, a fifth grade student, filled in this graphic organizer before writing a letter to the President of the United States requesting that sea turtles be protected. Tell them that they will want to use Felipe's graphic organizer page and his letter on page 45 to answer questions on both pages.

Test Item 1

Point out the missing picture in the graphic organizer. Say *There is a picture missing. Read what Felipe wrote about the sea turtles and look at the pictures.* Wait for students to read the graphic organizer. Point to test item 1. Say *Bubble in the choice for the picture that is missing.* Wait for students to bubble in their choice. Tell students to look at you when they are finished.

Test Item 2

Point to the blank line (2) and say *Write what Felipe forgot to write next to number 2.* Wait for students to write their answer. Tell students to look at you when they are finished.

Tell students that they are going to read the letter Felipe wrote after filling in the graphic organizer on page 44. Point to the missing sentences in the writing sample and say *There are two sentences missing.* Tell students to read the paragraph to see what is missing. Wait for students to read the writing sample. Remind students to use both the graphic organizer and the letter to answer test items 3–5.

Test Item 3

Point to test item 3 and say *Read the question and bubble in the choice for blank three.* Wait for students to mark their answers. Tell students to look at you when they are finished.

Test Item 4

Point to test item 4 and say *Read the question and bubble in the choice for blank four.* Wait for students to mark their answers. Tell students to look at you when they are finished.

Test Item 5

Point to test item 5 and say *Read the question and bubble in your answer choice.* Wait for students to mark their answers. Tell students to look at you when they are finished.

Test Item 6

Point to the sentences in the box at the bottom of the page. Say *Felipe wrote this letter about sea turtles.* Say *One of Felipe's sentences has a mistake.* Ask students to help Felipe fix his sentence. Say *Find the mistake and bubble in the choice for the sentence that would correct it.* Wait for students to mark their answer. Tell students to look at you when they are finished.

Unit 2 By the People

Vocabulary Ⓑ

Name _____   Date _____

Directions Look at the pictures. Listen to the question.
Bubble in the circle underneath the picture for your answer.

Sample

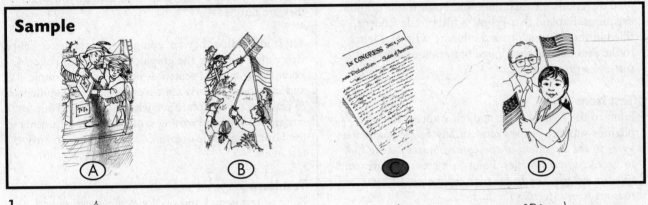

Ⓐ   Ⓑ   ●   Ⓓ

1

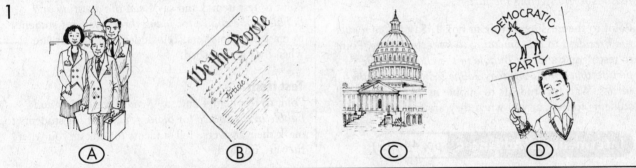

Ⓐ   Ⓑ   Ⓒ   Ⓓ

2

Ⓐ   Ⓑ   Ⓒ   Ⓓ

3

Ⓐ   Ⓑ   Ⓒ   Ⓓ

Name _____ Date _____

Directions Look at the pictures. Listen to the question. Bubble in the circle underneath the picture for your answer.

Sample

Ⓐ   **Ⓑ**

1

Ⓐ   Ⓑ

3

Ⓐ   Ⓑ

2

Ⓐ   Ⓑ

4

Ⓐ   Ⓑ

Name _____ Date _____

Directions Listen to the selection. Then read each question. Choose the best answer. Bubble in your answer.

Government Branches and Buildings

1 The U.S. government has three branches. Each branch has a different building.

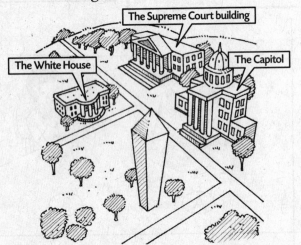

2 Congress is the Legislative Branch. Congress works in the Capitol. Congress votes on new laws called bills. Congress sends the bills to the Executive Branch.

3 The Executive Branch works in the White House. The President is the head of this branch.

4 The Judicial Branch works in the Supreme Court building. The Supreme Court Justices decide what the laws mean.

Unit 2 By the People

Name _____ Date _____

1 Where does the Legislative Branch work?

Capitol
(A)

Supreme Court building
(B)

White House
(C)

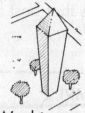
Washington Monument
(D)

2 Which picture answers the question: Where does the President work?

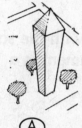
(A)

(B)

(C)

(D)

3 Which word is a proper noun?

grass
(A)

Washington, D.C.
(B)

road
(C)

tree
(D)

4 Where does Congress send bills after they vote?

to the Executive Branch
(A)

to the Judicial Branch
(B)

to the Capitol
(C)

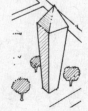
to the Supreme Court
(D)

Unit 2 By the People

Name _____ Date _____

> **Directions** Read the sentence. Choose the word or words that best fit in the blank. Bubble in your answer.

SAMPLE

People from each _____ helped win the war.

- Ⓐ tax
- Ⓑ colony
- Ⓒ freedom
- Ⓓ pamphlet

---

1 The legislative branch has _____.

- Ⓐ King George
- Ⓑ Congress
- Ⓒ British soldier
- Ⓓ colony

2 The President is the head of the _____.

- Ⓔ executive branch
- Ⓕ Constitution
- Ⓖ political party
- Ⓗ bill

3 United States citizens have _____ because of the Constitution.

- Ⓐ British soldiers
- Ⓑ bills
- Ⓒ rights
- Ⓓ independence

4 A group of people with the same ideas about government is a _____.

- Ⓔ political party
- Ⓕ veto
- Ⓖ bill
- Ⓗ citizen

5 The judicial branch has the _____.

- Ⓐ Boston Tea Party
- Ⓑ bill
- Ⓒ political party
- Ⓓ Supreme Court

Unit 2 By the People

Grammar ❶

Name _____ Date _____

Directions Read the sentence. Choose the word or words that best fit in the blank. Bubble in your answer.

SAMPLE

Where _____ **Mr. Ting going?**

- Ⓐ was
- Ⓑ do
- Ⓒ have
- Ⓓ does

1 **Susita likes pink shells, _____ Marco likes white shells.**

- Ⓐ if
- Ⓑ but
- Ⓒ from
- Ⓓ when

2 **The book that Pedro reads is _____.**

- Ⓔ a place
- Ⓕ a person
- Ⓖ a thing
- Ⓗ an idea

3 **Monique has the right _____ safe.**

- Ⓐ feel
- Ⓑ feels
- Ⓒ is feeling
- Ⓓ to feel

4 **_____ horse jumps high.**

- Ⓔ Azim's
- Ⓕ Azims'
- Ⓖ Azimses
- Ⓗ Azim

5 **The canoe _____ quiet on the water.**

- Ⓐ are
- Ⓑ is
- Ⓒ has
- Ⓓ am

Name _____ Date _____

Directions Read the selection. Then read each question. Choose the best answer. Bubble in your answer.

Government Branches and Buildings

What do you know about the government's three branches? Each branch has a different job. Each branch works in different buildings.

Congress, the Legislative Branch, works in the Capitol and votes on new laws called bills. Congress sends the bills to the Executive Branch.

The Executive Branch works in the White House. The White House, the heart of our country, helps guide us. The President is the head of this branch.

The Judicial Branch works in the Supreme Court building. The Supreme Court Justices decide what laws mean.

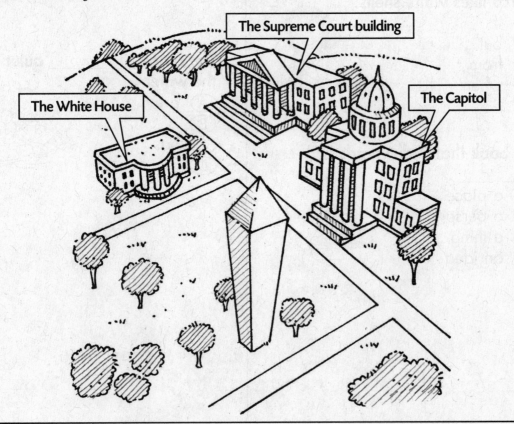

The Supreme Court building

The White House

The Capitol

Name _____ Date _____

1 **Look at the chart. Which word goes in the chart?**
   - Ⓐ government
   - Ⓑ White House
   - Ⓒ Washington, D.C.
   - Ⓓ laws

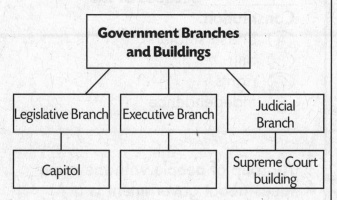

Government Branches and Buildings

Legislative Branch   Executive Branch   Judicial Branch

Capitol   Supreme Court building

2 **Where does Congress send bills after it votes?**
   - Ⓔ to the Executive Branch
   - Ⓕ to the Judicial Branch
   - Ⓖ to the Capitol
   - Ⓗ to the Supreme Court

3 **What is a question that you could ask about this sentence:** *The Supreme Court Justices decide what laws mean?*
   - Ⓐ Where is the Capitol?
   - Ⓑ How big is Washington, D.C.?
   - Ⓒ How do the Supreme Court Justices decide what laws mean?
   - Ⓓ Who is in the Executive branch?

4 **Which phrase is a metaphor?**
   - Ⓔ votes on new laws
   - Ⓕ the government's three branches
   - Ⓖ in the Supreme Court building
   - Ⓗ the heart of our country

5 **Which word is a proper noun?**
   - Ⓐ branch
   - Ⓑ work
   - Ⓒ law
   - Ⓓ Congress

6 **What is one question that you could ask after you have read this passage?**
   - Ⓔ Who was the first President of the United States?
   - Ⓕ Is Virginia far from Washington, D.C.?
   - Ⓖ How many people work for each branch of the government?
   - Ⓗ Are there many trees near the buildings?

Name _____ Date _____

Directions Read the sentence. Choose the word or words that best fit in the blank. Bubble in your answer.

SAMPLE

People from each _____ helped win the war.
Ⓐ tax
Ⓑ colony
Ⓒ freedom
Ⓓ pamphlet

---

1 The legislative branch has

_____.
Ⓐ King George
Ⓑ Congress
Ⓒ British soldier
Ⓓ colony

2 The President is the head of the

_____.
Ⓔ executive branch
Ⓕ Constitution
Ⓖ political party
Ⓗ bill

3 United States citizens have _____ because of the Constitution.
Ⓐ British soldiers
Ⓑ bills
Ⓒ rights
Ⓓ independence

4 A group of people with the same ideas about government is a

_____.
Ⓔ political party
Ⓕ veto
Ⓖ bill
Ⓗ citizen

5 The judicial branch has the

_____.
Ⓐ Boston Tea Party
Ⓑ bill
Ⓒ political party
Ⓓ Supreme Court

Unit 2 By the People

Grammar Ⓐ

Name _____ Date _____

Directions Read the sentence. Choose the word or words that best fit in the blank. Bubble in your answer.

SAMPLE

Where _____ Mr. Ting going?

Ⓐ was
Ⓑ do
Ⓒ have
Ⓓ does

---

1 Susita likes pink shells, _____ Marco likes white shells.

Ⓐ if
Ⓑ but
Ⓒ from
Ⓓ when

2 The book that Pedro reads is _____.

Ⓔ a place
Ⓕ a person
Ⓖ a thing
Ⓗ an idea

3 Monique has the right _____ safe.

Ⓐ feel
Ⓑ feels
Ⓒ is feeling
Ⓓ to feel

4 _____ horse jumps high.

Ⓔ Azim's
Ⓕ Azims'
Ⓖ Azimses
Ⓗ Azim

5 The canoe _____ quiet on the water.

Ⓐ are
Ⓑ is
Ⓒ has
Ⓓ am

Name _____ Date _____

Directions Read the selection. Then read each question. Choose the best answer. Bubble in your answer.

Government Branches and Buildings

What do you know about the Legislative Branch, the Judicial Branch, and the Executive Branch of the government? Each branch has a different job, but within each branch, its workers do similar work. Where do they work? They work in three different buildings or workplaces.

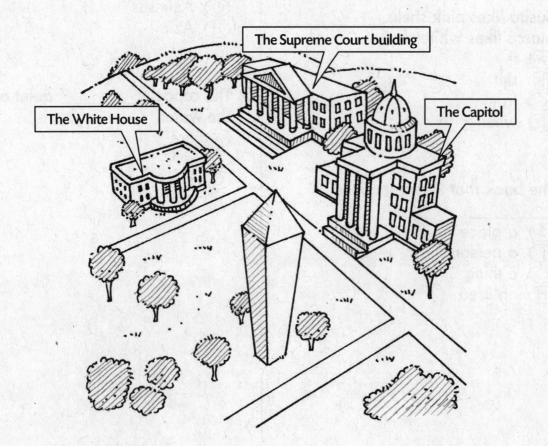

The Supreme Court building

The White House

The Capitol

Name _____ Date _____

The Capitol is the building where the Legislative Branch, or Congress, works. Congress votes on new laws called bills. Congress sends the new laws to the Executive Branch.

The building called the White House is where the Executive Branch works. The White House is the heart of our country. The President, head of the Executive Branch, and his staff work to enforce our laws and guide our country.

The Supreme Court building is the workplace for the Judicial Branch. The Supreme Court Justices listen to cases and decide what laws mean.

Name _____ Date _____

1 **Look at the chart. Which word goes in the chart?**
- Ⓐ government
- Ⓑ White House
- Ⓒ Washington, D.C.
- Ⓓ laws

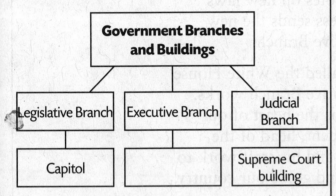

Government Branches and Buildings

Legislative Branch | Executive Branch | Judicial Branch

Capitol | | Supreme Court building

2 **Where does Congress send bills after it votes?**
- Ⓔ to the Executive Branch
- Ⓕ to the Judicial Branch
- Ⓖ to the Capitol
- Ⓗ to the Supreme Court

3 **What is a question that you could ask about this sentence: *The Supreme Court Justices listen to cases and decide what laws mean?***
- Ⓐ Where is the Capitol?
- Ⓑ How big is Washington, D.C.?
- Ⓒ How do the Supreme Court Justices decide what laws mean?
- Ⓓ Who is in the Executive Branch?

4 **Which phrase is a metaphor?**
- Ⓔ votes on new laws
- Ⓕ the government's three branches
- Ⓖ in the Supreme Court building
- Ⓗ the heart of our country

5 **Which word is a proper noun?**
- Ⓐ branch
- Ⓑ work
- Ⓒ law
- Ⓓ Congress

6 **What is one question you could ask after you have read this passage?**
- Ⓔ Who was the first President of the United States?
- Ⓕ Is Virginia far from Washington, D.C.?
- Ⓖ How many people work for each branch of the government?
- Ⓗ Are there many trees near the buildings?

Writing

Name _____   Date _____

Directions Look at the graphic organizer and student sample writing on page 45. Then answer the questions.

Date

> October 26, 2009

Greeting

> Dear Mr. President:

Body

Request	Please protect the sea turtles.	
1		**Detail** Please sign the bill to protect sea turtles.
		People walk on the turtles' eggs.
		Pollution on the beach also hurts the sea turtles. Please help save them!

Closing

> 2 _____
> Felipe Alvarez

---

1 Which picture best fits in box 1?

Ⓐ   Ⓑ

2 Fill in blank 2.

Name _____   Date _____

October 26, 2009

Dear Mr. President:

   The sea turtles need your help. Please sign the bill to protect them.
(3) _____ People step on the eggs. (4) _____
Please protect the sea turtles. They really need your help!

                                        Sincerely,

                                        Felipe Alvarez

---

3 **Which sentence best fits blank 3?**
   Ⓐ It's fun to play in the sand.
   Ⓑ Beaches need warning signs that say "Protected for Sea Turtles."
   Ⓒ I will visit Washington, D.C., in the summer.

4 **Which sentence best fits blank 4?**
   Ⓐ Polluted water and sand also hurt the turtles.
   Ⓑ We saw a whale yesterday.
   Ⓒ The turtles are very hungry.

5 **Which sentence in the letter best decribes Felipe's request?**
   Ⓐ Please protect the sea turtles.
   Ⓑ Please help the whales.
   Ⓒ People step on the eggs.

Please sign the bill to protect the sea turtles. The sea turtles needs your help, Mr. President!

---

6 **What would make the second sentence in the box above correct?**
   Ⓐ The sea turtles need your help, Mr. President!
   Ⓑ The sea turtles has your help, Mr. President!
   Ⓒ The sea turtles needed your help, Mr. President!

Beginning

Student _____   Teacher _____

Test Section	Skills Tested	Item Number	Total Scores	Reteaching Tools (For additional reteaching activities, see p. T14)
VOCABULARY *Date Tested:* _____	Words related to government	1, 2, 3	☐ × 9 points = **/27**	Newcomer Book TPR Cards Chant Posters Language Practice Concept Posters Game Academic Language Audio CD Builder
GRAMMAR *Date Tested:* _____	Subject-Verb Agreement with *have/be* Nouns	1, 3 2, 4	☐ × 8 points = **/32**	**Subject-Verb Agreement with *have/be*:** Teacher's Guide p. 74 **Nouns:** Teacher's Guide p. 84
READING *Date Tested:* _____	**Comprehension Strategy:** Asks Questions **Word Study:** Proper Nouns **Literary Analysis:** Sequence of Events	1, 2 3 4	☐ × 8 points = **/32**	**Comprehension Strategy:** Teacher's Guide p. 97 **Word Study:** Teacher's Guide p. 77 **Literary Analysis:** Teacher's Guide p. 97
WRITING *Date Tested:* _____	**Writing Form:** Business Letter	1	☐ × 9 points = **/9**	**Writing Form:** Teacher's Guide pp. 73, 75, 77, 79, 83, 85, 87

SKILLS TO BE DEVELOPED	UNIT 2 Total Score **/100**	COMMENTS
RETEACHING GROUP ASSIGNMENT		

| WRITING COMPOSITION EVALUATION

Date Tested:
_____ | Obtain individual student writing sample—Teacher's Guide, Week 4 Lesson 4, p. 113 | Figure score using pp. A14–A16

Composite Score ☐ | See appropriate mini-lessons in the *Writing Resource Guide* and Shared Writing Lessons in the Teacher's Guide, pp. 73, 75, 77, 79, 83, 85, 87 |

Student Profile | Unit 2 Progress Test

Intermediate/Advanced

Student _____

Teacher _____

Test Section	Skills Tested	Item Number	Total Scores	Reteaching Tools (For additional reteaching activities, see p. T14)
VOCABULARY *Date Tested:* _____	Words related to government	1, 2, 3, 4, 5	☐ x 4 points = **/20**	Newcomer Book TPR Cards Chant Posters Language Practice Concept Posters Game Academic Language Audio CD Builder

GRAMMAR
 	
Date Tested:
 	
_____
	Sentence Combining with *and* and *but*
	Nouns
	Have the right + Infinitive
	Possessives
	Subject-Verb Agreement with *have/be*
		1
		
		2
		3
		
		4
		5
			☐
			x
			4 points
			=
			/20
				Sentence Combining with *and* and *but*:
				  Teacher's Guide p. 111
				Nouns:
				  Teacher's Guide p. 84
				Have the right + Infinitive:
				  Teacher's Guide p. 72
				Possessives:
				  Teacher's Guide p. 102
				Subject-Verb Agreement with *have/be*:
				  Teacher's Guide p. 74

READING
 	
Date Tested:
 	
_____
	Nonfiction Text Feature: Charts
	Literary Analysis: Sequence of Events; Metaphor
	Comprehension Strategy: Asks Questions
	Word Study: Proper Nouns
		1
		
		2, 4
		
		3, 6
		
		5
			☐
			x
			5 points
			=
			/30
				Nonfiction Text Feature:
				  Teacher's Guide p.87
				Literary Analysis:
				  Teacher's Guide p. 79, 87
				Comprehension Strategy:
				  Teacher's Guide p. 97
				Word Study:
				  Teacher's Guide p. 89

WRITING
 	
Date Tested:
 	
_____
	Writing Form: Business Letter
	Written Convention: Subject-Verb Agreement
		1, 2, 3, 4, 5
		6
			☐
			x
			5 points
			=
			/30
				Writing Form:
				  Teacher's Guide pp. 73, 75, 77, 79, 83, 85, 87
				Written Convention:
				  Teacher's Guide p. 87

SKILLS TO BE DEVELOPED **RETEACHING GROUP ASSIGNMENT**	**UNIT 2** **Total** **Score** **/100**	**COMMENTS**
WRITING COMPOSITION EVALUATION *Date Tested:* _____	Obtain individual student writing sample—Teacher's Guide, Week 4 Lesson 4, p. 113	Figure score using pp. A14–A16 **Composite Score** ☐	See appropriate mini-lessons in the *Writing Resource Guide* and Shared Writing Lessons in the Teacher's Guide, pp. 73, 75, 77, 79, 83, 85, 87.

© 2010 Rigby®, an imprint of HMH Supplemental Publishers Inc. All rights reserved.

Name _____ Date _____

Things I Know About Reading in English!

When I read I ask questions about what I'm reading.

Yes   Sometimes   Not Yet

When I read I can put events in the order they happened.

Yes   Sometimes   Not Yet

Texts I Can Read in English!

Freedom

The Constitution and Our

Government

My Goals:

_____

_____

_____

Things I Can Say in English!

I can talk about government in English.

Yes   Sometimes   Not Yet

I can use nouns correctly.

Yes   Sometimes   Not Yet

My Goals:

_____

_____

_____

Things I Know About Writing in English!

I can use a graphic organizer to plan my business letter.

Yes   Sometimes   Not Yet

My Goals:

_____

_____

_____

Unit 3
Progress Test

Teacher Directions

Unit 3 Progress Test

Now Hear This!

Remind students that this is a test. Tell them that they will complete one test item at a time and that you will read directions for each question.

Sample

Distribute the test page. Point to the sample box. Tell students to look at the pictures in the box as you say and point to each picture: *This picture shows a* political party. *This picture shows the* Constitution. *This picture shows* Congress. *This picture shows a* veto. Ask *Which picture shows a* political party? Wait for students to respond orally. Say *Bubble* A *is filled in because we were looking for a* political party.

Test Items

Say the following directions for each test item. Wait for students to bubble in their choice. Tell students to look at you when they are finished with each item.

1. Have students point to item number 1 and say *Look at the pictures in row one. Which picture shows* vibration? Tell students to bubble in the circle under the picture that shows *vibration.*

2. Have students point to item number 2 and say *Look at the pictures in row two. Which picture shows* percussion instruments? Tell students to bubble in the circle under the picture that shows *percussion instruments.*

3. Have students point to item number 3 and say *Look at the pictures in row three. Which picture shows* volume? Tell students to bubble in the circle under the picture that shows *volume.*

Remind students that this is a test. Tell them that they will complete one test item at a time and that you will read directions for each question.

Sample

Distribute the test page. Point to the sample sentence in the box. Tell students that one word is missing in the sentence. Say *Read this sentence with me. The* blank *is part of the judicial branch.* Say *Now we will*

read the sentence again with each answer choice to see which one best fits in the blank. The Congress *is part of the judicial branch.* The legislative branch *is part of the judicial branch.* The Supreme Court *is part of the judicial branch.* The government *is part of the judicial branch.* Ask *Which answer would make sense to put in the blank?* Wait for students to respond orally. Tell students that bubble choice C is filled in because *The Supreme Court is part of the judicial branch* is the correct choice.

Test Items

Say the following directions for each test item. Then wait for students to bubble in their choice. Tell students to look at you when they are finished with each item.

1. Say *Point to test item 1. Read the sentence with me. She could feel the* blank *as the train moved past.* Then say *Read the sentence again and try each word in the blank.* Wait for students to read. Then say *Bubble in the choice for the word that goes in the blank.*

2. Say *Point to test item 2. Read the sentence with me. A guitar is one of the* blank. Then say *Read the sentence again and try each word in the blank.* Wait for students to read. Then say *Bubble in the choice for the word that goes in the blank.*

3. Say *Point to test item 3. Read the sentence with me. He put a blanket over his drum to* blank *the sound.* Then say *Read the sentence again and try each word in the blank.* Wait for students to read. Then say *Bubble in the choice for the word that goes in the blank.*

4. Say *Point to test item 4. Read the sentence with me. A drum is one of the* blank. Then say *Read the sentence again and try each word in the blank.* Wait for students to read. Then say *Bubble in the choice for the word that goes in the blank.*

5. Say *Point to test item 5. Read the sentence with me. When you listen to music, you can change the* blank. Then say *Read the sentence again and try each word in the blank.* Wait for students to read. Then say *Bubble in the choice for the word that goes in the blank.*

Grammar

Now Hear This!

Beginning p. 55

Remind students that this is a test. Tell them that they will complete one test item at a time and that you will read directions for each question.

Sample

Distribute the test page. Point to the sample box. Tell students to look at the pictures in the box as you say and point to each picture: *This picture shows a girl going for a walk. This picture shows a man and a woman walking their dogs. Which picture shows* They walk? Wait for students to respond orally. Say *Bubble* B *is filled in because we were looking for the picture that shows* They walk.

Test Items

Say the following directions for each test item. Wait for students to bubble in their choice. Tell students to look at you when they are finished with each item.

1. Have students point to item number 1 and say *Look at the pictures. Which picture shows* They are busy? Tell students to bubble in the choice under the picture that shows *They are busy.*

2. Have students point to item number 2 and say *Look at the pictures. Which picture shows* He writes? Tell students to bubble in the choice under the picture that shows *He writes.*

3. Have students point to item number 3 and say *Look at the pictures. Which picture shows* This food is good? Tell students to bubble in the choice under the picture that shows *This food is good.*

4. Have students point to item number 4 and say *Look at the pictures. Which picture shows* Mario swims well? Tell students to bubble in the choice under the picture that shows *Mario swims well.*

Intermediate p. 59   **Advanced** p. 63

Remind students that this is a test. Tell them that they will complete one test item at a time and that you will read directions for each question.

Sample

Distribute the test page. Point to the sample sentence in the box. Tell students that one word is missing in the sentence. Say *Read this sentence with me. All the children* blank *a song together.* Say *Now we will read the sentence again with each choice to see which one best fits in the blank. All the children* is sing *a song together. All the children* was sing *a song together. All the children* sing *a song together. All the children* sings *a song together.* Ask *Which word would make sense to put in the blank?* Wait for students to respond orally. Tell students that bubble C is filled in because *All the children* sing *a song together* is the correct choice.

Test Items

Say the following directions for each test item. Wait for students to bubble in their choice. Tell students to look at you when they are finished with each item.

1. Say *Point to test item 1. Read the sentence with me. María starts to dance* blank *she hears the music.* Then say *Read the sentence again and try each word in the blank.* Wait for students to read. Then say *Bubble in the choice for the word that goes in the blank.*

2. Say *Point to test item 2. Read the sentence with me. Arturo* blank *the book.* Then say *Read the sentence again and try each word in the blank.* Wait for students to read. Then say *Bubble in the choice for the word that goes in the blank.*

3. Say *Point to test item 3. Read the sentence with me. You can buy a glass of lemonade* blank *you have ten cents.* Then say *Read the sentence again and try each word in the blank.* Wait for students to read. Then say *Bubble in the choice for the word that goes in the blank.*

4. Say *Point to test item 4. Read the sentence with me. The children* blank *happy.* Then say *Read the sentence again and try each word in the blank.* Wait for students to read. Then say *Bubble in the choice for the word that goes in the blank.*

5. Say *Point to test item 5. Read the sentences with me. Hurry, Alfredo! If you swim fast, you* blank *win the race!* Then say *Read the sentence again and try each word in the blank.* Wait for students to read. Then say *Bubble in the choice for the word that goes in the blank.*

Reading

Now Hear This!

Beginning pp. 56–57

Remind students that this is a test. Tell them that they will complete one test item at a time and that you will read directions for each question.

Passage

Distribute the reading passage on page 56. Have students point to the pictures in the boxes. Explain that the story is about a girl who once lived in Puerto Rico and a singing frog called a coqui (*ko-kee*). Ask students to follow along as you read the passage aloud. Point to each illustration as you read the corresponding text.

Say *Listen as I read the story* "**The Happy Girl and the Singing Coqui.**"

1. *Look at picture 1.* Years ago a girl lived here on the island of Puerto Rico. She seemed happy.

2. *Look at picture 2.* A coqui sang, "Ko-kee," in her garden every night.

3. *Look at Picture 3.* One night she did not hear the frog sing. She was sad.

4. *Look at picture 4.* Weeks later, a friend came to the garden.
"Here is a coqui," he said.
"I hear it singing!" she said. She was happy.

Test Items

Distribute test page 57. Say the following directions for each test item. Read aloud the question and choices. Give students time to read and look at the pictures. Then wait for students to bubble in their choice. Tell students to look at you as they finish each item.

1. Say *Point to test item 1. Look at the pictures. Read the question with me. What made the "ko-kee" sound? Bubble in the choice that shows what made the "ko-kee" sound.*

2. Say *Point to test item 2. Look at the pictures. Read the question with me. What made the girl happy? Bubble in the choice that tells what made the girl happy.*

3. Say *Point to test item 3. Look at the pictures. Read the question with me. Why did the friend bring the girl a coqui? Bubble in the choice that tells why the friend brought the girl a coqui.*

4. Say *Point to test item 4. Look at the pictures. Read the question with me. Which sentence has a linking verb? Bubble in the choice that shows a sentence with a linking verb.*

Intermediate pp. 60–61
Advanced pp. 64–66

Remind students that this is a test. Explain that they will read the passage on their own and complete the test items.

Passage

Distribute the reading passage. Have students point to the passage. Point to the illustration. Tell students that they are going to read about a happy girl who lived on the island of Puerto Rico and a singing frog called a coqui *(ko-kee)*. Ask students to read the passage independently and to look at you when they are finished.

Test Items

Distribute the test page. Remind students that they will look back at the passage for help in answering questions.

Tell students that they will complete the test by themselves.

Beginning p. 68

Remind students that this is a test. Tell them that they will complete one test item and that you will read directions for each question. Explain that Jinwon, a fifth grader, filled in this chart before she wrote a poem about going to a parade.

Test Item 1

Point to the Descriptive Words spaces. Point to the pictures and say *These are some things that Jinwon saw and heard at the parade.* Point to the two pictures and filled-in descriptive words. Say *Jinwon wrote* heard the triangles go ding-ding *and* heard the fire engine go clang-clang. Point to the missing picture in box 1. Ask *What else did Jinwon see and hear at the parade.* Point to test item 1. Say *Bubble in the choice for the picture that shows one of the things Jinwon saw and heard at the parade.* Wait for students to bubble in their choice. Tell students to look at you when they are finished.

Intermediate/Advanced pp. 68–69

Remind students that this is a test. Tell them that they will complete one test item at a time and that you will read directions for each question. Point to the graphic organizer. Explain that Jinwon, a fifth grader, filled in this chart before she wrote a poem describing a parade on page 69. Tell them that they will want to use the graphic organizer page and the paragraph that Jinwon wrote to answer the questions on both pages.

Test Item 1

Point out the missing picture in the graphic organizer. Say *There is a picture missing. Read what Jinwon wrote about going to a parade and look at the pictures.* Wait for students to read the graphic organizer. Point to test item 1. Say *Bubble in the choice for the picture that is missing.* Wait for students to bubble in their choice. Tell students to look at you when they are finished.

Test Item 2

Point to the blank lines (2) in the graphic organizer and say *Write the descriptive words that Jinwon forgot to write.* Wait for students to write what goes on the blank line. Tell students to look at you when they are finished.

Tell students that they are going to read the paragraph that Jinwon wrote after filling in the graphic organizer on page 68. Point to the missing sentences in the writing sample and say *There are two sentences missing. Read the paragraph to see what is missing.* Wait for students to read the writing sample. Tell students to look at you when they are finished. Remind students to use both the graphic organizer and the paragraph to answer test items 3, 4 and 5.

Test Item 3

Point to test item 3 and say *Read the question and bubble in the choice for blank three.* Wait for students to mark their answers. Tell students to look at you when they are finished.

Test Item 4

Point to test item 4 and say *Read the question and bubble in the choice for blank four.* Wait for students to mark their answers. Tell students to look at you when they are finished.

Test Item 5

Point to test item 5 and say *Read the question and bubble in your choice.* Wait for students to mark their answers. Tell students to look at when they are finished.

Test Item 6

Point to the sentences in the box at the bottom of the page. Say *Jinwon's friend, Juanita, wrote these sentences about going to the parade. One of Juanita's sentences has a mistake. Find the mistake and bubble in the choice for the sentence that would correct it.* Wait for students to mark their answers. Tell students to look at you when they are finished.

Unit 3 Now Hear This!

Vocabulary Ⓑ

Name _____   Date _____

Directions Look at the pictures. Listen to the question. Bubble in the circle underneath the picture for your answer.

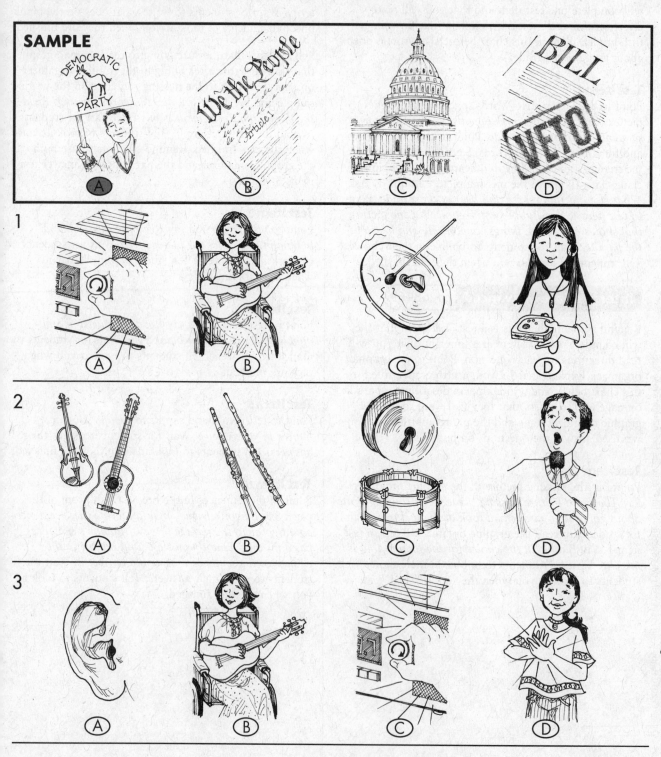

SAMPLE

A   B   C   D

1   A   B   C   D

2   A   B   C   D

3   A   B   C   D

Unit 3   Now Hear This!

Grammar  B

Name _____   Date _____

Directions Look at the pictures. Listen to the question. Bubble in the circle underneath the picture for your answer.

SAMPLE

Ⓐ   Ⓑ

1

Ⓐ   Ⓑ

3

Ⓐ   Ⓑ

2

Ⓐ   Ⓑ

4

Ⓐ   Ⓑ

Name _____   Date _____

Directions Listen to the selection. Then read each
question. Choose the best answer. Bubble in your answer.

The Happy Girl and the Singing Coqui

1   Years ago, a girl lived
here on the island of
Puerto Rico. She seemed
happy.

2   A coqui sang, "Ko-kee," in her
garden every night.

3   One night, she did not hear
the frog sing. She was sad.

4   Weeks later, a friend came to the
garden. "Here is a coqui," he said.

"I hear it singing!" she said.
She was happy.

Name _____   Date _____

1 What made the "ko-kee" sound?

bird
Ⓐ

tree
Ⓑ

flower
Ⓒ

coqui
Ⓓ

2 What made the girl happy?

A tree
Ⓐ

The coqui
Ⓑ

A bird
Ⓒ

A flower
Ⓓ

3 Why did the friend bring the girl a coqui?

She was happy.
Ⓐ

She was sad.
Ⓑ

She lived on
an island.
Ⓒ

A coqui sang
in her garden.
Ⓓ

4 Which sentence has a linking verb?

She lived on
an island.
Ⓐ

The night was dark.
Ⓑ

Her frog
didn't sing.
Ⓒ

She did not
like the garden.
Ⓓ

Unit 3   Now Hear This!

Vocabulary ❶

Name _____   Date _____

Directions Read the sentence. Choose the word or words that best fit in the blank. Bubble in your answer.

SAMPLE

The _____ is part of the judicial branch.

(A) Congress
(B) legislative branch
(C) Supreme Court
(D) government

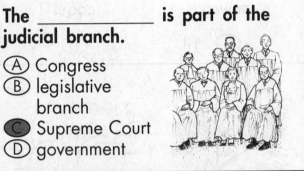

---

1 She could feel the _____ as the train moved past.

(A) sound waves
(B) pitch
(C) echo
(D) vibrations

2 A guitar is one of the _____.

(E) string instruments
(F) brass instruments
(G) wind instruments
(H) percussion instruments

---

3 He put a blanket over his drum to _____ the sound.

(A) amplify
(B) reflect
(C) echo
(D) muffle

4 A drum is one of the _____.

(E) string instruments
(F) wind instruments
(G) percussion instruments
(H) brass instruments

5 When you listen to music, you can change the _____.

(A) echo
(B) eardrum
(C) volume
(D) beat

Name _____ Date _____

Directions Read the sentence. Choose the word or words that best fit in the blank. Bubble in your answer.

SAMPLE

All the children _____ a song together.

- Ⓐ is sing
- Ⓑ was sing
- Ⓒ sing
- Ⓓ sings

1 María starts to dance _____ she hears the music.

- Ⓐ before
- Ⓑ later
- Ⓒ was
- Ⓓ when

2 Arturo _____ the book.

- Ⓔ cooks
- Ⓕ reads
- Ⓖ swims
- Ⓗ eats

3 You can buy a glass of lemonade _____ you have ten cents.

- Ⓐ if
- Ⓑ were
- Ⓒ would
- Ⓓ must

4 The children _____ happy.

- Ⓔ is
- Ⓕ was
- Ⓖ look
- Ⓗ if

5 Hurry, Alfredo! If you swim fast, you _____ win the race!

- Ⓐ may not
- Ⓑ could
- Ⓒ could not
- Ⓓ must

Name _____ Date _____

Directions Read the selection. Then read each question.
Choose the best answer. Bubble in your answer.

The Happy Girl and the Singing Coqui

Years ago, a girl lived in Puerto Rico. She seemed happy.

A small coqui frog sang "Ko-kee" in her garden every night.

One night, she did not hear the frog sing. She was very sad. Her parents and friends were worried. Nothing helped.

Weeks later, a friend came to the garden. "Here is a coqui like yours," he said.

"I hear it singing!" she said. She was happy again.

Name _____ Date _____

1 **What sound did the coqui make at night?**
  (A) cooking
  (B) ko-kee
  (C) cookie
  (D) cake-cake

2 **Why did the girl's friend bring her a coqui?**
  (E) She was happy.
  (F) She had parents.
  (G) She lived in Puerto Rico.
  (H) She was sad.

3 **What is the conflict in the story?**
  (A) The girl's parents didn't sing a song.
  (B) The girl's coqui didn't sing a song.
  (C) The boy with the coqui didn't sing a song.
  (D) The girl's friends didn't sing a song.

4 **Which one is correct?**
  (E) "Hear is a coqui like yours," he said.
  (F) A girl lived hear in Puerto Rico.
  (G) "I hear it singing!" she said.
  (H) She did not here the frog sing.

5 **Why did the girl become happy again?**
  (A) She lived in Puerto Rico.
  (B) She had friends.
  (C) She had a new coqui.
  (D) She liked her garden.

6 **What did the new coqui do?**
  (E) It sang.
  (F) It flew away.
  (G) It was silent.
  (H) It hopped away.

Name _____ Date _____

Directions Read the sentence. Choose the word or words that best fit in the blank. Bubble in your answer.

SAMPLE

The _____ is part of the judicial branch.

Ⓐ Congress
Ⓑ legislature branch
● Supreme Court
Ⓓ goverment

---

1 She could feel the _____ as the train moved past.
Ⓐ sound waves
Ⓑ pitch
Ⓒ echo
Ⓓ vibrations

2 A guitar is one of the _____.
Ⓔ string instruments
Ⓕ brass instruments
Ⓖ wind instruments
Ⓗ percussion instruments

3 He put a blanket over his drum to _____ the sound.
Ⓐ amplify
Ⓑ reflect
Ⓒ echo
Ⓓ muffle

4 A drum is one of the _____.
Ⓔ string instruments
Ⓕ wind instruments
Ⓖ percussion instruments
Ⓗ brass instrument

5 When you listen to music, you can change the _____.
Ⓐ echo
Ⓑ eardrum
Ⓒ volume
Ⓓ beat

Name _____ Date _____

Directions Read the sentence. Choose the word or words that best fit in the blank. Bubble in your answer.

SAMPLE

All the children _____ a song together.

- Ⓐ is sing
- Ⓑ was sing
- Ⓒ sing
- Ⓓ sings

---

1 María starts to dance _____ she hears the music.
- Ⓐ before
- Ⓑ later
- Ⓒ was
- Ⓓ when

2 Arturo _____ the book.
- Ⓔ cooks
- Ⓕ reads
- Ⓖ swims
- Ⓗ eats

3 You can buy a glass of lemonade _____ you have ten cents.
- Ⓐ if
- Ⓑ were
- Ⓒ would
- Ⓓ must

4 The children _____ happy.
- Ⓔ is
- Ⓕ was
- Ⓖ look
- Ⓗ if

5 Hurry, Alfredo! If you swim fast, you _____ win the race!
- Ⓐ may not
- Ⓑ could
- Ⓒ could not
- Ⓓ must

Name _____   Date _____

Directions Read the selection. Then read each question.
Choose the best answer. Bubble in your answer.

The Happy Girl and the Singing Coqui

Years ago, on the island of Puerto Rico, there lived a girl named
Ramona. She seemed happy.

A small coqui frog sang in her garden every night. The frog sang
"Ko-kee, ko-kee," all night long.

One night, she did not hear the frog's song. She seemed very sad.
Her parents and friends were worried. Nothing helped.

Weeks later, as the sun went down, Ramona was in her garden when she heard singing.

Her friend Jorge came into the garden. On his shoulder sat a coqui that looked and sang just like hers! "Here is a coqui like yours," Jorge said.

"I hear it singing!" said Ramona. Finally, Ramona was happy again.

Unit 3 Now Hear This!

Name _____ Date _____

1 **What sound did the coqui make at night?**
- (A) cooking
- (B) ko-kee
- (C) cookie
- (D) cake-cake

2 **Why did Ramona's friend bring her a coqui?**
- (E) Ramona was happy.
- (F) Ramona had parents.
- (G) Ramona lived in Puerto Rico.
- (H) Ramona was sad.

3 **What is the conflict in the story?**
- (A) Ramona's parents didn't sing a song.
- (B) The coqui didn't sing a song.
- (C) Jorge didn't sing a song.
- (D) Ramona's friends didn't sing a song.

4 **Which one is correct?**
- (E) "Hear is a coqui like yours," Jorge said.
- (F) Ramona lived hear in Puerto Rico.
- (G) "I hear it singing!" said Ramona.
- (H) She did not here the frog's song.

5 **Why did Ramona become happy again?**
- (A) She lived in Puerto Rico.
- (B) She had friends.
- (C) She had a new coqui.
- (D) She liked her garden.

6 **What did the new coqui do?**
- (E) It sang.
- (F) It flew away.
- (G) It was silent.
- (H) It hopped away.

Writing

Name _____ Date _____

Directions Look at the following graphic organizer and student sample writing on page 69. Then answer the following questions.

	Descriptive Words
	2 _____ _____ _____
1	heard the triangles go ding-ding
	heard the fire engine go clang-clang

---

1 Which picture best fits in box 1?

Ⓐ

Ⓑ

2 Fill in blank 2.

Unit 3 Now Hear This!

Writing ❶Ⓐ

Name _____ Date _____

The big parade came down the street.

(3) _____.

The drums made a boom-boom kind of beat.

(4) _____.

When the sounds began to fade,

We knew it was the end of the parade.

---

3 **Which sentence best fits blank 3?**
- Ⓐ The triangles made a ding-ding sound.
- Ⓑ The library was quiet today.
- Ⓒ We went shopping last week.

4 **Which sentence best fits blank 4?**
- Ⓐ We read lots of books about parks.
- Ⓑ The store sold a lot of toys that made sounds.
- Ⓒ The fire engine's clang-clang was all around.

5 **Which two words from the poem rhyme?**
- Ⓐ street and fade
- Ⓑ beat and parade
- Ⓒ street and beat

We heard sounds at the parade. What did you hear at the parade

---

6 **What would make the second sentence in the box above correct?**
- Ⓐ What did you hear at the parade!
- Ⓑ What did you hear at the parade?
- Ⓒ What did you hear at the parade.

Beginning

Student _____   Teacher _____

Item Analysis

Test Section	Skills Tested	Item Number	Total Scores	Reteaching Tools (For additional reteaching activities, see p. T14)
VOCABULARY *Date Tested:* _____	Words related to sound	1, 2, 3	☐ × 9 points = /27	Newcomer Book Academic Language Builder Song Charts TPR Cards Chant Posters Language Practice Game Concept Posters Audio CD

GRAMMAR
Date Tested:
_____
	Linking Verbs
	
	Regular Verbs
		1, 3
		
		2, 4
			☐
			×
			8 points
			=
			/32
				Linking Verbs:
				  Teacher's Guide p. 132
				
				Regular Verbs:
				  Teacher's Guide p. 142

READING
Date Tested:
_____
	Literary Analysis:
	  Onomatopoeia
	Comprehension Strategy: Monitor Understanding
	Word Study:
	  Linking Verbs
		1
		
		2, 3
		
		4
			☐
			×
			8 points
			=
			/32
				Literary Analysis:
				  Teacher's Guide p. 137
				Comprehension Strategy:
				  Teacher's Guide p. 154
				Word Study:
				  Teacher's Guide p. 157

WRITING *Date Tested:* _____	**Writing Form:** Poem	1	☐ × 9 points = /9	Writing Form: Teacher's Guide pp. 131, 133, 135, 137, 141, 143, 145

SKILLS TO BE DEVELOPED		UNIT 3	COMMENTS
		Total Score	
RETEACHING GROUP ASSIGNMENT		/100	

| WRITING COMPOSITION EVALUATION
Date Tested:
_____ | Obtain individual student writing sample — Teacher's Guide, Week 4, Lesson 4, p. 171 | Figure score using pp. A14–A16

Composite Score ☐ | See appropriate mini-lessons in the *Writing Resource Guide* and Shared Writing lessons in the Teacher's Guide, pp. 131, 133, 135, 137, 141, 143, 145 |

Intermediate/Advanced

Student _____   Teacher _____

Item Analysis

Test Section	Skills Tested	Item Number	Total Scores	Reteaching Tools (For additional reteaching activities, see p. T14)
VOCABULARY *Date Tested:* _____	Words related to sound	1, 2, 3, 4, 5	☐ x 4 points = /20	Newcomer Book Academic Language Builder Song Charts Chant Posters TPR Cards Concept Posters Language Practice Game Audio CD

GRAMMAR
 	
 Date Tested:
 _____
	Clauses with *when* and *if*
	 Regular Verbs
	 Linking Verbs
	 Helping Verbs
		1, 3
		
		 2
		 4
		 5
			☐
			 x
			 4 points
			 =
			 /20
				Clauses with *when* and *if:*
				   Teacher's Guide p. 130
				 Regular Verbs:
				   Teacher's Guide p. 142
				 Linking Verbs:
				   Teacher's Guide p. 132
				 Helping Verbs:
				   Teacher's Guide p. 168

READING
 	
 Date Tested:
 _____
	Literary Analysis:
	   Onomatopoeia;
	   Plot, Conflict, and
	   Sequence of Events
	 Comprehension Strategy: Monitor Understanding
	 Word Study:
	   Homonyms
		1; 3, 6
		
		 2, 5
		
		 4
			☐
			 x
			 5 points
			 =
			 /30
				Literary Analysis:
				   Teacher's Guide pp. 137, 147
				 Comprehension Strategy:
				   Teacher's Guide p. 154
				 Word Study:
				   Teacher's Guide p. 135

WRITING
 	
 Date Tested:
 _____
	Writing Form: Poem
	
	 Written Convention:
	   Sentence Types
		1, 2
		 3, 4, 5
		 6
			☐
			 x
			 5 points
			 =
			 /30
				Writing Form:
				   Teacher's Guide pp. 131, 133, 135,
				   137, 141, 143, 145
				
				 Written Convention:
				   Teacher's Guide p. 145

SKILLS TO BE DEVELOPED		UNIT 3 **Total Score**	COMMENTS
RETEACHING GROUP ASSIGNMENT		/100	

| WRITING COMPOSITION EVALUATION

 Date Tested:
 _____ | Obtain individual student writing sample — Teacher's Guide, Week 4, Lesson 4, p. 171 | Figure score using pp. A14–A16

 Composite Score ☐ | See appropriate mini-lessons in the *Writing Resource Guide* and Shared Writing lessons in the Teacher's Guide, pp. 131, 133, 135, 137, 141, 143, 145 |

Name _____   Date _____

Things I Know About Reading in English!

When I read I make sure I understand what I've read.

Yes   **Sometimes**   **Not Yet**

When I read I can find examples of onomatopoeia.

Yes   **Sometimes**   **Not Yet**

Texts I Can Read in English!

The Loveliest Song of All

Animals Use Sound

My Goals:

_____
_____
_____

Things I Can Say in English!

I can talk about sounds in English.

Yes   **Sometimes**   **Not Yet**

I can use linking verbs in English.

Yes   **Sometimes**   **Not Yet**

My Goals:

_____
_____

Things I Know About Writing in English!

I can use a graphic organizer to plan my poem.

Yes   **Sometimes**   **Not Yet**

My Goals:

_____
_____

Unit 4
Progress Test

Unit 4 Progress Test
In the Deep

Beginning p. 78

Remind students that this is a test. Tell them that they will complete one test item at a time and that you will read directions for each question.

Sample

Distribute the test page. Point to the sample box. Tell students to look at the pictures in the box as you say and point to each picture: *This picture shows* percussion instruments. *This picture shows* wind instruments. *This picture shows* string instruments. *This picture shows* brass instruments. Ask *Which picture shows* string instruments? Wait for students to respond orally. Say *Bubble C is filled in because we were looking for* string instruments.

Test Items

Say the following directions for each test item. Then wait for students to bubble in their choice. Tell students to look at you when they are finished with each item.

1. Have students point to item number 1 and say *Look at the pictures in row one. Which picture shows an* environment? Tell students to bubble in the circle under the picture that shows an *environment*.

2. Have students point to item number 2 and say *Look at the pictures in row two. Which picture shows* coral? Tell students to bubble in the circle under the picture that shows *coral*.

3. Have students point to item number 3 and say *Look at the pictures in row three. Which picture shows* seaweed? Tell students to bubble in the circle under the picture that shows *seaweed*.

Intermediate p. 82   Advanced p. 86

Remind students that this is a test. Tell them that they will complete one test item at a time and that you will read directions for each question.

Sample

Distribute the test page. Point to the sample sentence in the box. Tell students that one word is missing in the sentence. Say *Read this sentence with me. The guitar is a* blank. Say *Now we will read the sentence again with each choice to see which one best fits in the blank. The guitar is a* wind instrument. *The guitar is a* brass instrument. *The guitar is a* percussion instrument. *The guitar is a* string instrument. Ask *Which words would*

make sense to put in the blank? Wait for students to respond orally. Tell students that bubble D is filled in because *The guitar is a string instrument* is the correct choice.

Test Items

Say the following directions for each test item. Then wait for students to bubble in their choice. Tell students to look at you when they are finished with each item.

1. Say *Point to test item 1. Read the sentence with me. Some ocean reefs are made from* blank.

   Then say *Read the sentence again and try each word in the blank.*

   Wait for students to read, then say *Bubble in the choice for the word that goes in the blank.*

2. Say *Point to test item 2. Read the sentences with me. Plants that live and grow in the water are called* blank.

   Then say *Read the sentences again and try each word in the blank.*

   Wait for students to read, then say *Bubble in the choice for the word that goes in the blank.*

3. Say *Point to test item 3. Read the sentence with me. Water, plants, and other fish are part of a fish's* blank.

   Then say *Read the sentence again and try each word in the blank.*

   Wait for students to read, then say *Bubble in the choice for the word that goes in the blank.*

4. Say *Point to test item 4. Read the sentence with me. Animals that live only in the ocean are called* blank *animals.*

   Then say *Read the sentence again and try each word in the blank.*

   Wait for students to read, then say *Bubble in the choice for the word that goes in the blank.*

5. Say *Point to test item 5. Read the sentence with me. Most ocean animals live under the* blank *of the water.*

   Then say *Read the sentence again and try each word in the blank.*

   Wait for students to read, then say *Bubble in the choice for the word that goes in the blank.*

Teacher Directions | Unit 4 Progress Test

Grammar

In the Deep

Beginning p. 79

Remind students that this is a test. Tell them that they will complete one test item at a time and that you will read directions for each question.

Sample

Distribute the test page. Point to the sample box. Tell students to look at the pictures in the box as you say and point to each picture: *This picture shows* The water feels cold. *This picture shows* The girl is beside the pool. *Which picture shows* The water feels cold? Wait for students to respond orally. Say *Bubble A is filled in because we were looking for the picture that shows* The water feels cold.

Test Items

Say the following directions for each test item. Then wait for students to bubble in their choice. Tell students to look at you when they are finished with each item.

1. Have students point to item number 1 and say *Look at the pictures. Which picture shows* He is eating his lunch now?

    Tell students to bubble in the circle under the picture that shows *He is eating his lunch now.*

2. Have students point to item number 2 and say *Look at the pictures. Which picture shows* This is a *big* boat?

    Tell students to bubble in the circle under the picture that shows *This is a* big *boat.*

3. Have students point to item number 3 and say *Look at the pictures. Which picture shows* We are shopping for our food?

    Tell students to bubble in the circle under the picture that shows *We are shopping for our food.*

4. Have students point to item number 4 and say *Look at the pictures. Which picture shows* This is a *round* toy?

    Tell students to bubble in the circle under the picture that shows *This is a* round *toy.*

Intermediate p. 83   Advanced p. 87

Remind students that this is a test. Tell them that they will complete one test item at a time and that you will read directions for each question.

Sample

Distribute the test page. Point to the sample sentence in the box. Tell students that one or two words are missing in the sentence. Say *Read this sentence with me. This* apple blank good. Say *Now we will read the sentence again with each answer choice to see which one best fits in the blank. This apple* is taste *good. This apple* were being *good. This apple* tastes *good. This apple* taste *good.* Ask *Which word or words would make sense to put in the blank?* Wait for students to respond orally. Tell students that bubble C is filled in because *This apple tastes good* is the correct choice.

Test Items

Say the following directions for each test item. Then wait for students to bubble in their choice. Tell students to look at you when they are finished with each item.

1. Say *Point to test item 1. Read the sentence with me. He* blank *his lunch now.* Then say *Read the sentence and try each answer choice in the blank.* Wait for students to read. Then say *Bubble in the choice for the answer that goes in the blank.*

2. Say *Point to test item 2. Read the sentence with me. This is a* blank *boat.* Then say *Read the sentence and try each answer choice in the blank.* Wait for students to read. Then say *Bubble in the choice for the answer that goes in the blank.*

3. Say *Point to test item 3. Read the sentence with me. We* blank *for our food.* Then say *Read the sentence and try each answer choice in the blank.* Wait for students to read. Then say *Bubble in the choice for the answer that goes in the blank.*

4. Say *Point to test item 4. Read the sentence with me. The ball is* blank. Then say *Read the sentence and try each answer choice in the blank.* Wait for students to read. Then say *Bubble in the choice for the answer that goes in the blank.*

5. Say *Point to test item 5. Read the sentence with me. I* blank *to read.* Then say *Read the sentence and try each answer choice in the blank.* Wait for students to read. Then say *Bubble in the choice for the answer that goes in the blank.*

Teacher Directions | Unit 4 Progress Test

Reading

In the Deep

Beginning pp. 80–81

Remind students that this is a test. Tell them that they will complete one test item at a time and that you will read directions for each question.

Passage

Distribute the reading passage on page 80. Have students point to the pictures in the boxes. Explain that fish that live in the Dark Zone have parts of their bodies that glow in the dark. Explain that this gives these types of fish a very scary appearance. Ask students to follow along as you read the passage aloud. Point to each illustration as you read the corresponding text.

Say *Listen as I read* **"The Anglerfish."**

1. *Look at picture 1.*   *The anglerfish lives deep in the ocean.*

   It has big, sharp, pointy teeth and a long hook.

2. *Look at picture 2.*   *The hook hangs in front of the anglerfish's mouth and glows in the dark ocean.*

   Bacteria make it glow.

3. *Look at picture 3.*   *Other fish like the glow.*

   They swim to the hook.

4. *Look at picture 4.*   *Then the anglerfish eats them. It gets a lot of food.*

   That fish is never hungry!

Test Items

Distribute test page 81. Say the following directions for each test item. Read aloud the question. Give students time to read and look at the pictures. Then wait for students to bubble in their choice. Tell students to look at you when they are finished with each item.

1. Say *Point to test item 1. Read the question with me. This story is about* blank. *Look at the pictures and read the answer choices. Bubble in the choice that tells what the story is about.*

2. Say *Point to test item 2. Read the question with me. What hangs in front of the anglerfish's mouth? Look at the pictures and read the answer choices. Bubble in the choice that tells what hangs in front of the anglerfish's mouth.*

3. Say *Point to test item 3. Read the question with me. Which words best describe the anglerfish's teeth? Look at the pictures and read the answer choices. Bubble in the choice that describes the anglerfish's teeth.*

4. Say *Point to test item 4. The anglerfish's mouth makes it look* blank. *Read the answer choices. Bubble in the choice that uses the correct prefix.*

Intermediate pp. 84–85
Advanced pp. 88–90

Remind students that this is a test. Explain that they will read the passage on their own and complete the test items.

Passage

Distribute the reading passages. Have students point to the passage. Point to the graphic in the passage. Explain that the graphic information goes with the passage and that they will read this as well as the passage. Tell students that they are going to read about a fish that lives in the Dark Zone called the anglerfish. Ask students to read the passage independently and to look at you when they are finished.

Test Items

Distribute the test pages. Remind students that they may look back at the passage for help in answering questions.

1. Say *Point to test item 1. Read the question with me. What is the most important thing to know about the anglerfish's hook? Read and bubble in the correct choice.* Wait for students to bubble in their choice. Tell students to look at you when they are finished.

2. Say *Point to item number 2. Look at the drawing of the anglerfish and the skateboard at the bottom of page 84. Read the question with me. Which sentence is true? Read and bubble in the choice that tells which sentence is true.* Wait for students to bubble in their choice. Tell students to look at you when they are finished.

Tell students to complete the rest of the test themselves.

In the Deep

Beginning p. 92

Remind students that this is a test. Tell them that they will complete one test item and that you will read directions for the question. Distribute test page 92. Point to the graphic organizer. Explain that Luisa, a fifth-grade student, filled in this chart before writing an observation log comparing and contrasting two kinds of fish.

Test Item 1

Point to the graphic organizer. Say *Luisa wants to write an observation log entry on two types of fish. She needs to fill out a compare/contrast chart about the two fish so that she can write the observation log entry. She put the name of one fish, the Siamese Fighting Fish, on one side of the chart.* Point to empty box 1 and say *One picture is missing.* Point to test item 1 and ask *Which picture best fits in box 1? Bubble in the picture that is missing.* Wait for students to bubble in their choice. Tell students to look at you when they are finished.

Intermediate/Advanced pp. 92–93

Remind students that this is a test. Tell them that they will complete one test item at a time and that you will read directions for each question. Distribute the test pages. Point to the graphic organizer. Explain to students that Luisa, a fifth-grade student, filled in this chart before writing the observation log entry comparing and contrasting two kinds of fish on page 93. Tell them that they will want to use the graphic organizer page and the paragraph that Luisa wrote to answer the questions on both pages.

Test Item 1

Tell students to read the graphic organizer. Point out the missing picture in box 1. Point to test item 1. Say *Bubble in the choice for the picture that best fits in box 1.* Wait for students to bubble in their choice. Tell students to look at you when they are finished.

Test Item 2

Point to the blank line (2) and say *Label the picture telling what the boxes in the second column show.* Wait for students to write their answer. Tell students to look at you when they are finished.

Tell students that they are going to read the paragraph that Luisa wrote after filling in the chart on page 92. Point to the missing sentences in the writing sample, and say *There are two sentences missing.* Tell students to read the paragraph to see what is missing. Wait for students to read the writing sample. Tell students to look at you when they are finished. Remind students to use both the graphic organizer and the paragraph to answer test items 3–5.

Test Item 3

Point to test item 3 and say *Read the question and bubble in the choice for blank three.* Wait for students to mark their answers. Tell students to look at you when they are finished.

Test Item 4

Point to test item 4 and say *Read the question and bubble in the choice for blank four.* Wait for students to mark their answers. Tell students to look at you when they are finished.

Test Item 5

Point to test item 5 and say *Read the question and bubble in the best answer choice.* Wait for students to mark their answers. Tell students to look at you when they are finished.

Test Item 6

Point to the sentences in the box at the bottom of the page. Say *Luisa's classmate, Victor, wrote these sentences in his journal entry.* Tell students *One of Victor's sentences has a mistake.* Ask students to help Victor fix his sentence. Say *Find the mistake and bubble in the choice for the correction that he should make.* Wait for students to mark their answers. Tell students to look at you when they are finished.

Name _____ Date _____

Directions Look at the pictures. Listen to the question.
Bubble in the circle underneath the picture for your answer.

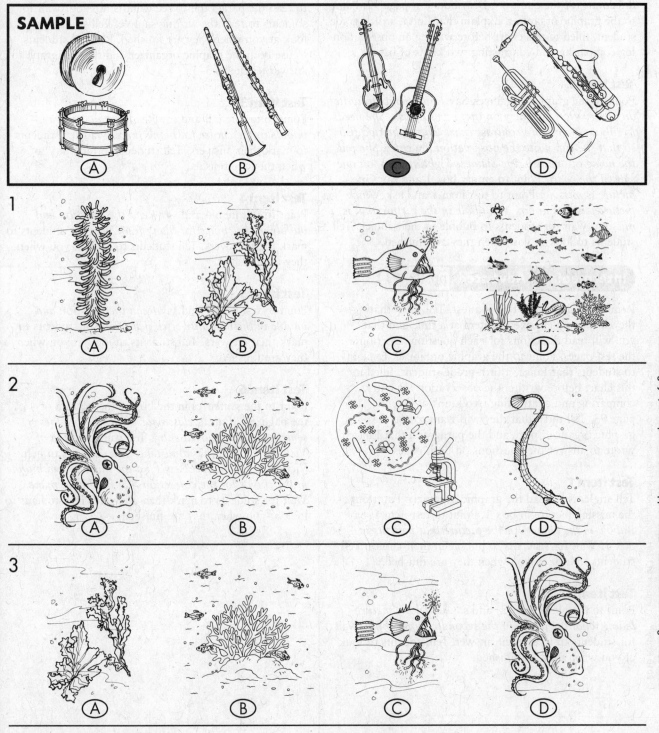

SAMPLE

Ⓐ Ⓑ Ⓒ Ⓓ

1 Ⓐ Ⓑ Ⓒ Ⓓ

2 Ⓐ Ⓑ Ⓒ Ⓓ

3 Ⓐ Ⓑ Ⓒ Ⓓ

Unit 4 In the Deep

Grammar Ⓑ

Name _____ Date _____

Directions Look at the pictures. Listen to the question. Bubble in the circle underneath the picture for your answer.

SAMPLE

Ⓐ Ⓑ

1

Ⓐ Ⓑ

3

Ⓐ Ⓑ

2

Ⓐ Ⓑ

4

 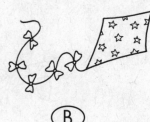

Ⓐ Ⓑ

Name _____   Date _____

Directions Listen to the selection. Then read each
question. Choose the best answer. Bubble in your answer.

The Anglerfish

1   The anglerfish lives deep in
    the ocean.

    It has big, sharp, pointy teeth
    and a long hook.

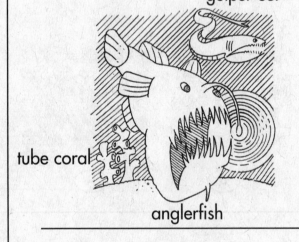

gulper eel

tube coral

anglerfish

2   The hook hangs in front of the
    anglerfish's mouth and glows in
    the dark ocean.

    Bacteria make it glow.

hook

3   Other fish like the glow.

    They swim to the hook.

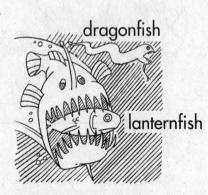

dragonfish

lanternfish

4   Then the anglerfish eats them.
    It gets a lot of food.

    That fish is never hungry!

Atolla jellyfish

Name _____ Date _____

1 This story is about _____.

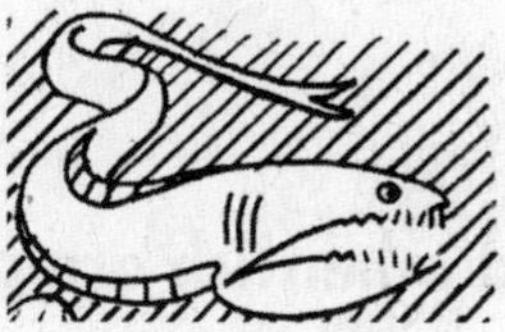

the gulper eel
Ⓐ

the anglerfish
Ⓑ

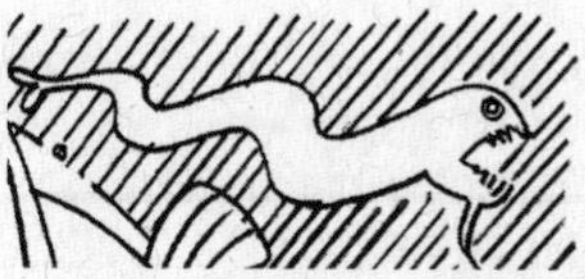

the dragonfish
Ⓒ

the Atolla jellyfish
Ⓓ

2 What hangs in front of the anglerfish's mouth?

a hook
Ⓐ

a coral
Ⓑ

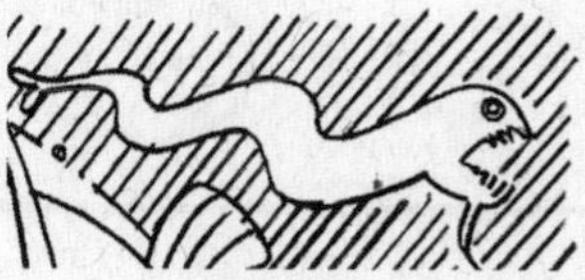

a dragonfish
Ⓒ

a jellyfish
Ⓓ

3 Which words best describe the anglerfish's teeth?

small
Ⓐ

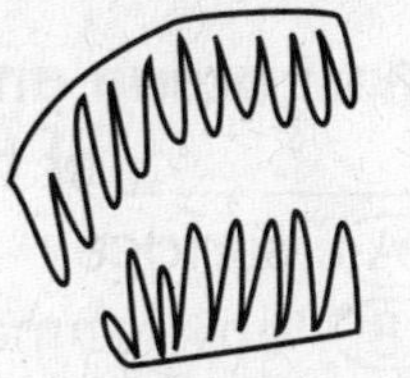

rounded and large
Ⓑ

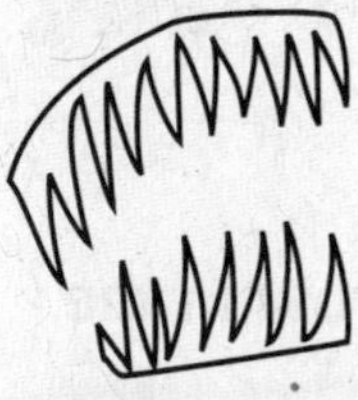

big, sharp, and pointy
Ⓒ

dark and small
Ⓓ

4 The anglerfish's mouth makes it look _____.

friendly
Ⓐ

unfriendly
Ⓑ

nonfriendly
Ⓒ

refriendly
Ⓓ

Unit 4 In the Deep

Vocabulary 1

Name _____ Date _____

Directions Read the sentences. Choose the word or words that best fit in the blank. Bubble in your answer.

SAMPLE

The guitar is a _____.
- Ⓐ wind instrument
- Ⓑ brass instrument
- Ⓒ percussion instrument
- ⬤ string instrument

---

1 Some ocean reefs are made from _____.
- Ⓐ salt water
- Ⓑ bacteria
- Ⓒ coral
- Ⓓ octopus

2 Plants that live and grow in the water are called _____.
- Ⓔ seaweed
- Ⓕ organism
- Ⓖ pipefish
- Ⓗ coral

3 Water, plants, and other fish are part of a fish's _____.
- Ⓐ life form
- Ⓑ depth
- Ⓒ salt water
- Ⓓ environment

4 Animals that live only in the ocean are called _____ animals.
- Ⓔ trench
- Ⓕ marine
- Ⓖ transparent
- Ⓗ surface

5 Most ocean animals live under the _____ of the water.
- Ⓐ surface
- Ⓑ environment
- Ⓒ zone
- Ⓓ trench

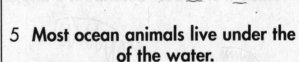

Name _____ Date _____

Directions Read the sentence. Choose the word or words that best fit in the blank. Bubble in your answer.

SAMPLE

This apple _____ good.

Ⓐ is taste
Ⓑ were being
🄲 tastes
Ⓓ taste

---

1 He _____ his lunch now.

Ⓐ are eating
Ⓑ is eating
Ⓒ eating
Ⓓ am eating

2 This is a _____ boat.

Ⓔ go
Ⓕ man
Ⓖ big
Ⓗ there

---

3 We _____ for our food.

Ⓐ are shopping
Ⓑ is shopping
Ⓒ are shop
Ⓓ am shopping

4 The ball is _____.

Ⓔ square
Ⓕ round
Ⓖ smart
Ⓗ funny

5 I _____ to read.

Ⓐ is learning
Ⓑ learns
Ⓒ to learn
Ⓓ am learning

Name _____ Date _____

Directions Read the selection. Then read each question.
Choose the best answer. Bubble in your answer.

A Fish of the Dark Zone

The anglerfish has a large head and many big, sharp, pointy teeth.
It lives in the ocean in the Dark Zone, where there is no light. The
anglerfish also has a glowing hook hanging in front of its mouth.
Bacteria make the hook glow. The hook is so bright, other fish swim
near it. Then the anglerfish opens its large mouth and snaps its jaws
over the fish. The hook helps the anglerfish to get food easily.

Zones of the Sea

Sunlight Zone 0–600 ft. (0–200 m)

Twilight Zone 600–3,300 ft. (200–1,000 m)

Dark Zone 3,300–16,000 ft. (1,000–5,000 m)

The anglerfish can eat this
large lanternfish.

36 inches

30 inches

Unit 4 In the Deep

Name _____ Date _____

1 **What is the most important thing to know about the anglerfish's hook?**
  - (A) It helps the fish get food easily.
  - (B) It is pretty.
  - (C) Bacteria makes the hook glow.
  - (D) It works in the Dark Zone of the ocean.

2 **Which sentence is true?**
  - (E) The anglerfish is bigger than the skateboard.
  - (F) The anglerfish and the skateboard are the same size.
  - (G) The skateboard is bigger than the anglerfish.
  - (H) The anglerfish is smaller than the skateboard.

3 **This passage is about _____.**
  - (A) the ocean's Dark Zone
  - (B) dragonfish
  - (C) the anglerfish
  - (D) oceans

4 **Which words best create a picture in your mind of the anglerfish's teeth?**
  - (E) swimming in the deep
  - (F) glowing like a light bulb
  - (G) sharp and pointy as knives
  - (H) big and rounded

5 **What information in the selection is interesting but not important?**
  - (A) The angler fish has a glowing hook.
  - (B) The hook makes fish swim near the fish's mouth.
  - (C) The hook helps the anglerfish get food.
  - (D) Bacteria makes the hook glow.

6 **The anglerfish's mouth makes it look _____.**
  - (E) friendly
  - (F) refriendly
  - (G) nonfriendly
  - (H) unfriendly

Unit 4   In the Deep

Vocabulary Ⓐ

Name _____ Date _____

Directions Read the sentences. Choose the word or words that best fit in the blank. Bubble in your answer.

SAMPLE

The guitar is a _____.
- Ⓐ wind instrument
- Ⓑ brass instrument
- Ⓒ percussion instrument
- Ⓓ string instrument

---

1 Some ocean reefs are made from _____.
- Ⓐ salt water
- Ⓑ bacteria
- Ⓒ coral
- Ⓓ octopus

2 Plants that live and grow in the water are called _____.
- Ⓔ seaweed
- Ⓕ organism
- Ⓖ pipefish
- Ⓗ coral

3 Water, plants, and other fish are part of a fish's _____.
- Ⓐ life form
- Ⓑ depth
- Ⓒ salt water
- Ⓓ environment

4 Animals that live only in the ocean are called _____ animals.
- Ⓔ trench
- Ⓕ marine
- Ⓖ transparent
- Ⓗ surface

5 Most ocean animals live under the _____ of the water.
- Ⓐ surface
- Ⓑ environment
- Ⓒ zone
- Ⓓ trench

Name _____   Date _____

Directions Read the sentence. Choose the word or words that best fit in the blank. Bubble in your answer.

SAMPLE

This apple _____ good.
- Ⓐ is taste
- Ⓑ were being
- Ⓒ tastes
- Ⓓ taste

1 **He _____ his lunch now.**
- Ⓐ are eating
- Ⓑ is eating
- Ⓒ eating
- Ⓓ am eating

2 **This is a _____ boat.**
- Ⓔ go
- Ⓕ man
- Ⓖ big
- Ⓗ there

3 **We _____ for our food.**
- Ⓐ are shopping
- Ⓑ is shopping
- Ⓒ are shop
- Ⓓ am shopping

4 **The ball is _____.**
- Ⓔ square
- Ⓕ round
- Ⓖ smart
- Ⓗ funny

5 **I _____ to read.**
- Ⓐ is learning
- Ⓑ learns
- Ⓒ to learn
- Ⓓ am learning

Name _____ Date _____

Directions Read the selection. Then read each question.
Choose the best answer. Bubble in your answer.

A Fish of the Dark Zone

Light does not shine in the Dark Zone of the ocean. In order to adapt to their environment, most creatures in the Dark Zone glow. This glow is called bioluminescence. The anglerfish is a fish that lives in the Dark Zone. It has an oversized head and sharp teeth.

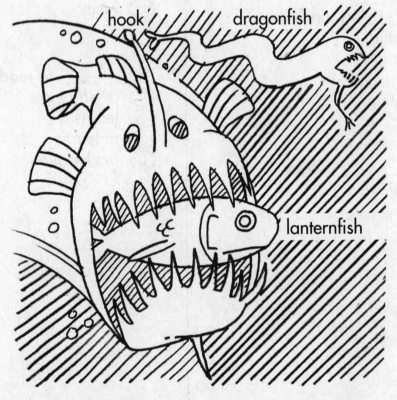

The anglerfish can eat this large lanternfish.

Name _____   Date _____

The anglerfish has a glowing hook hanging from a fin in front of its mouth. The fin is decorated with branches and bacteria that help create the glowing color.

The hook is so bright that it attracts prey. The prey comes closer until the anglerfish opens its large mouth and snaps it up. Anglerfish can reach a length of 3 feet (1 meter) and weigh as much as 20 pounds (9 kilograms).

Zones of the Sea

Sunlight Zone 0–600 ft. (0–200 m)

Twilight Zone 600–3,300 ft. (200–1,000 m)

Dark Zone 3,300–16,000 ft. (1,000–5,000 m)

36 inches

30 inches

Name _____ Date _____

1 **What is the most important thing to know about the anglerfish's hook?**
   Ⓐ It helps the fish get food easily.
   Ⓑ It is pretty.
   Ⓒ Bacteria makes the hook glow.
   Ⓓ It works in the Dark Zone of the ocean.

2 **Which sentence is true?**
   Ⓔ The anglerfish is bigger than the skateboard.
   Ⓕ The anglerfish and the skateboard are the same size.
   Ⓖ The skateboard is bigger than the anglerfish.
   Ⓗ The anglerfish is smaller than the skateboard.

3 **This passage is about _____.**
   Ⓐ the ocean's Dark Zone
   Ⓑ dragonfish
   Ⓒ the anglerfish
   Ⓓ oceans

4 **Which words best create a picture in your mind of the anglerfish's teeth?**
   Ⓔ swimming in the deep
   Ⓕ glowing like a light bulb
   Ⓖ sharp and pointy as knives
   Ⓗ big and rounded

5 **What information in the selection is interesting but not important?**
   Ⓐ The angler fish has a glowing hook.
   Ⓑ The hook makes fish swim near the fish's mouth.
   Ⓒ The hook helps the anglerfish get food.
   Ⓓ Bacteria makes the hook glow.

6 **The anglerfish's mouth makes it look _____.**
   Ⓔ friendly
   Ⓕ refriendly
   Ⓖ nonfriendly
   Ⓗ unfriendly

Writing

Unit 4   In the Deep

Writing Ⓑ❶Ⓐ

Name _____   Date _____

Directions Look at the following graphic organizer and student sample writing on page 93. Then answer the questions.

Siamese Fighting Fish

2 _____

1

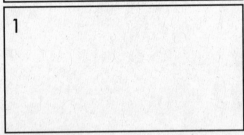

1 **Which picture best fits in box 1?**

2 **Fill in blank 2.**

Ⓐ   Ⓑ

Name _____ Date _____

Monday, 8:30 A.M.

The Kuhli Loach and the Siamese Fighting Fish are alike in one way, but mostly they are different. (3) _____. The Kuhli Loach never comes to the top of the tank. The Kuhli Loach eats at the bottom of the tank. Both fish have fins, but the Siamese Fighting Fish has bigger fins. The Kuhli Loach has whiskers. (4) _____. In conclusion, Siamese Fighting Fish and Kuhli Loaches are more different than they are alike.

---

3 Which sentence best fits blank 3?
- Ⓐ It's fun to have an aquarium.
- Ⓑ The Kuhli Loach is prettier than the Siamese Fighting Fish.
- Ⓒ Both fish are very hungry, but the Siamese Fighting Fish eats at the top.

4 Which sentence best fits blank 4?
- Ⓐ In contrast, the Siamese Fighting Fish has no whiskers.
- Ⓑ Finally, the Kuhli Loach swims at the top and the bottom.
- Ⓒ However, both fish are fast swimmers.

5 Which statement might not have been made if the fish were observed on a different day?
- Ⓐ The Kuhli Loach never comes to the top of the tank.
- Ⓑ Both fish have fins, but the Siamese Fighting Fish has bigger fins.
- Ⓒ The Kuhli Loach has whiskers.

The Kuhli Loach is fun to watch, and the Siamese Fighting Fish is even more fun. I love observing fish.

---

6 What correction should be made to the first sentence in the box above?
- Ⓐ change *more* to *most*
- Ⓑ change *and* to *but*
- Ⓒ change *more* to *less*

Student Profile | Unit 4 Progress Test

Beginning

Student _____   Teacher _____

Test Section	Skills Tested	Item Number	Total Scores	Reteaching Tools (For additional reteaching activities, see p. T14)
VOCABULARY Date Tested: _____	Words related to the sea	1, 2, 3	☐ x 9 points = /27	Newcomer Book TPR Cards Chant Posters Vocabulary Cards Concept Posters Language Practice Game Academic Language Builder Audio CD
GRAMMAR Date Tested: _____	Present Continuous Adjectives	1, 3 2, 4	☐ x 8 points = /32	**Present Continuous:** Teacher's Guide p. 188 **Adjectives:** Teacher's Guide p. 190
READING Date Tested: _____	**Comprehension Strategy:** Determine Importance **Literary Analysis:** Descriptive Language and Imagery **Word Study:** Prefix un-	1, 2 3 4	☐ x 8 points = /32	**Comprehension Strategy:** Teacher's Guide p. 212 **Literary Analysis:** Teacher's Guide p. 195 **Word Study:** Teacher's Guide pp. 193, 205, 215
WRITING Date Tested: _____	**Writing Form:** Observation Log	1	☐ x 9 points = /9	**Writing Form:** Teacher's Guide pp. 189, 191, 193, 195, 199, 201, 203

SKILLS TO BE DEVELOPED RETEACHING GROUP ASSIGNMENT	**UNIT 4** **Total Score** /100	**COMMENTS**

| **WRITING COMPOSITION EVALUATION**
 Date Tested: _____ | Obtain individual student writing sample — Teacher's Guide, Week 4, Lesson 4, p. 229 | Figure score using pp. A14–A16

 Composite Score ☐ | See appropriate mini-lessons in the *Writing Resource Guide* and Shared Writing lessons in the Teacher's Guide, pp. 189, 191, 193, 195, 199, 201, 203. |

Intermediate/Advanced

Student _____

Teacher _____

Test Section	Skills Tested	Item Number	Total Scores	Reteaching Tools (For additional reteaching activities, see p. T14)
VOCABULARY Date Tested: _____	Words related to the sea	1, 2, 3, 4, 5	☐ x 4 points = /20	Newcomer Book — TPR Cards — Chant Posters — Vocabulary Cards — Concept Posters — Language Practice Game — Academic Language Builder — Audio CD
GRAMMAR Date Tested: _____	Present Continuous — Adjectives	1, 3, 5 — 2, 4	☐ x 4 points = /20	**Present Continuous:** Teacher's Guide p. 188 — **Adjectives:** Teacher's Guide p. 190
READING Date Tested: _____	**Comprehension Strategy:** Determine Importance — **Nonfiction Text Feature:** Scale Drawings — **Literary Analysis:** Descriptive Language and Imagery — **Word Study:** Prefix *un-*	1, 3, 5 — 2 — 4 — 6	☐ x 5 points = /30	**Comprehension Strategy:** Teacher's Guide p. 212 — **Nonfiction Text Feature:** Teacher's Guide p. 205 — **Literary Analysis:** Teacher's Guide p. 195 — **Word Study:** Teacher's Guide pp. 193, 205, 215
WRITING Date Tested: _____	**Writing Form:** Observation Log — **Written Convention:** Sentence Combining with *and* and *but*	1, 2, 3, 4, 5 — 6	☐ x 5 points = /30	**Writing Form:** Teacher's Guide pp. 189, 191, 193, 195, 199, 201, 203 — **Written Convention:** Teacher's Guide p. 203

SKILLS TO BE DEVELOPED	UNIT 4 Total Score /100	COMMENTS
RETEACHING GROUP ASSIGNMENT		

| **WRITING COMPOSITION EVALUATION** Date Tested: _____ | Obtain individual student writing sample — Teacher's Guide, Week 4, Lesson 4, p. 229 | Figure score using pp. A14–A16 — **Composite Score** ☐ | See appropriate mini-lessons in the *Writing Resource Guide* and Shared Writing lessons in the Teacher's Guide, pp. 189, 191, 193, 195, 199, 201, 203. |

Unit 4   In the Deep

Self-Assessment

Name _____   Date _____

Things I Know About Reading in English!

I can tell what is important when I read.

Yes   **Sometimes**   **Not Yet**

I can use a scale drawing to compare the sizes of things.

Yes   **Sometimes**   **Not Yet**

Texts I Can Read in English!

Octopus Food Fight

Life Deep Down

_____

My Goals:

_____

_____

_____

Things I Can Say in English!

I can talk about things that live in the ocean in English.

Yes   **Sometimes**   **Not Yet**

I can talk about things that are happening right now in English.

Yes   **Sometimes**   **Not Yet**

My Goals:

_____

_____

_____

Things I Know About Writing in English!

I can use a graphic organizer to plan my observation log.

Yes   **Sometimes**   **Not Yet**

My Goals:

_____

_____

_____

Unit 5
Progress Test

Beginning p. 102

Remind students that this is a test. Tell them that they will complete one test item at a time and that you will read directions for each question.

Sample

Distribute the test page. Point to the sample box. Tell students to look at the pictures in the box as you say and point to each picture: *This picture shows* seaweed. *This picture shows* tubeworms. *This picture shows* plants. *This picture shows* algae. Ask *Which picture shows* seaweed? Wait for students to respond orally. Say *Bubble* A *is filled in because we were looking for* seaweed.

Test Items

Say the following directions for each test item. Then wait for students to bubble in their choice. Tell students to look at you when they are finished with each item.

1. Have students point to item number 1 and say *Look at the pictures in row one. Which picture shows a* wagon?

   Tell students to bubble in the circle under the picture that shows a *wagon*.

2. Have students point to item number 2 and say *Look at the pictures in row two. Which picture shows a* pioneer?

   Tell students to bubble in the circle under the picture that shows a *pioneer*.

3. *Have students point to item number 3 and say Look at the pictures in row three. Which picture shows a* mission?

   Tell students to bubble in the circle under the picture that shows a *mission*.

Intermediate p. 106   **Advanced** p. 110

Remind students that this is a test. Tell them that they will complete one test item at a time and that you will read directions for each question.

Sample

Distribute the test page. Point to the sample sentences in the box. Tell students that one word is missing in the first sentence. Say *Read these sentences with me. Some reefs in tropical waters are made from* blank. Say *Now we will read the sentence again with each choice to see which one best fits in the blank. Some reefs in tropical waters are made from* coral. *Some reefs in tropical waters are made*

from anglerfish. *Some reefs in tropical waters are made from* bacteria. *Some reefs in tropical waters are made from* salt water. Ask *Which word would make sense to put in the blank?* Wait for students to respond orally. Tell students that bubble A is filled in because *Some reefs in tropical waters are made from coral* is the correct choice.

Test Items

Say the following directions for each test item. Then wait for students to bubble in their choice. Tell students to look at you when they are finished with each item.

1. Say *Point to test item 1. Read the sentence with me. It was difficult to* blank *the settlers as they traveled west.*

   Then say *Read the sentence again and try each word or words in the blank.*

   Wait for students to read. Say *Bubble in the choice for the word or words that go in the blank.*

2. Say *Point to test item 2. Read the sentence with me. The* blank *rolled along under the moonlight.*

   Then say *Read the sentence again and try each word in the blank.*

   Wait for students to read. Say *Bubble in the choice for the word that goes in the blank.*

3. Say *Point to test item 3. Read the sentence with me. A person who settled in the West was known as a* blank.

   Then say *Read the sentence again and try each word in the blank.*

   Wait for students to read. Say *Bubble in the choice for the word that goes in the blank.*

4. Say *Point to test item 4. Read the sentence with me. The movement of people to the West was called* blank.

   Then say *Read the sentence again and try each word or words in the blank.*

   The movement of the people to the west was called blank.

5. Say *Point to test item 5. Read the sentence with me. A Spanish church in the Southwest is called a* blank.

   Then say *Read the sentence again and try each word or words in the blank.*

   Wait for students to read. Say *Bubble in the choice for the word or words that go in the blank.*

Teacher Directions | Unit 5 Progress Test

Grammar

A Growing Nation

Beginning p. 103

Remind students that this is a test. Tell them that they will complete one test item at a time and that you will read directions for each question.

Sample

Distribute the test page. Point to the sample box. Tell students to look at the pictures in the box as you say and point to each picture: *This picture shows* He is reaching for his lunch. *This picture shows* He is eating his lunch now. *Which picture shows* He is eating his lunch now? Wait for students to respond orally. Say *Bubble* B *is filled in because we were looking for the picture that shows* He is eating his lunch now.

Test Items

Say the following directions for each test item. Then wait for students to bubble in their choice. Tell students to look at you when they are finished with each item.

1. Have students point to item number 1 and say *Look at the pictures. Listen. Which picture shows* Mr. Ortiz is in his truck? Tell students to bubble in the circle under the picture that shows *Mr. Ortiz is in his truck.*

2. Have students point to item number 2 and say *Look at the pictures. Listen. Which picture shows* Mrs. Kwan does her work? Tell students to bubble in the circle under the picture that shows *Mrs. Kwan does her work.*

3. Have students point to item number 3 and say *Look at the pictures. Listen. Which picture shows* They are under the water? Tell students to bubble in the circle under the picture that shows *They are under the water.*

4. Have students point to item number 4 and say *Look at the pictures. Listen. Which picture shows* Look at Father and Mother. They sit in their chairs? Tell students to bubble in the circle under the picture that shows *Look at Father and Mother. They sit in their chairs.*

Intermediate p. 107   Advanced p. 111

Remind students that this is a test. Tell them that they will complete one test item at a time and that you will read directions for each question.

Sample

Distribute the test page. Point to the sample sentence in the box. Tell students that one or more words are missing in the sentence. Say *Read this sentence with me.* The ball is blank. Say *Now we will read the sentence again with each choice to see which one best fits in the blank.* The ball is bounce. The ball is round. The ball is under. The ball is happily. Ask *Which answer would make sense to put in the blank?* Wait for students to respond orally. Tell students that bubble *B* is filled in because *The ball is round* is the correct choice.

Test Items

Say the following directions for each test item. Then wait for students to bubble in their choice. Tell students to look at you when they are finished with each item.

1. Say *Point to test item 1. Read the sentence with me.* Jorge takes a bite of blank apple. Then say *Read the sentence and try each choice in the blank.* Wait for students to read, then say *Bubble in the choice for the answer that goes in the blank.*

2. Say *Point to test item 2. Read the sentence with me.* It blank all day yesterday. Then say *Read the sentence and try each choice in the blank.* Wait for students to read, then say *Bubble in the choice for the answer that goes in the blank.*

3. Say *Point to test item 3. Read the sentence with me.* The girl blank a glass of lemonade. Then say *Read the sentence and try each choice in the blank.* Wait for students to read, then say *Bubble in the choice for the answer that goes in the blank.*

4. Say *Point to test item 4. Read the sentences with me.* Now we are eating. Earlier, we blank. Then say *Read the sentences and try each choice in the blank.* Wait for students to read, then say *Bubble in the choice for the answer that goes in the blank.*

5. Say *Point to test item 5. Read the sentence with me.* Luis hit the baseball blank the fence. Then say *Read the sentence and try each choice in the blank.* Wait for students to read, then say *Bubble in the choice for the answer that goes in the blank.*

Reading

A Growing Nation

Beginning pp. 104–105

Remind students that this is a test. Tell them that they will complete one test item at a time and that you will read directions for each question.

Passage

Distribute the reading passage on page 104. Have students point to the pictures in the boxes. Explain that pioneers traveled from the eastern half of the United States to the western half of the United States by covered wagon. Ask students to follow along as you read the passage aloud. Point to each illustration as you read the corresponding text.

Say *Listen as I read the story* **"A Journey Through the Mountains."**

1. *Look at Picture 1.* It is the fall of 1818. Winter is coming.
   Mr. Smith's group is near the mountains.

2. *Look at Picture 2.* Clouds Dancing shows the group a mountain pass.
   Mr. Smith is a good leader. Clouds Dancing is a good guide.

3. *Look at Picture 3.* It is January in 1819.
   They go along the Platte River.

4. *Look at Picture 4.* The trip is long.
   By the spring of 1819, they will be in Oregon.

Test Items

Distribute test page 105. Say the following directions for each test item. Read aloud the questions. Give students time to read and look at pictures. Then wait for students to bubble in their choice. Tell students to look at you when they are finished with each item.

1. Say *Point to test item 1. Read the question with me. In the sentence* They go along the Platte River, *who are they? Look at the pictures and read the answer choices. Bubble in the choice that tells who they are.*

2. Say *Point to test item 2. When I read this question, try to make a connection to your own life to help you find the best answer: Clouds Dancing acts most like a blank. Bubble in the choice that tells what kind of person Clouds Dancing acts like.*

3. Say *Point to test item 3. Read the question with me. Mr. Smith is a good leader. Clouds Dancing is a good blank. Bubble in the choice that tells about Clouds Dancing.*

4. Say *Point to test item 4. Use what you know about the seasons to answer this question. During which season would travel be most difficult? Bubble in the choice that tells when travel would be most difficult.*

Intermediate pp. 108–109
Advanced pp. 112–114

Remind students that this is a test. Explain that they will read the passage on their own before completing the test items.

Passage

Distribute the reading passages. Point to the passage. Tell students that they are going to read about how pioneers, while they traveled west, used Native American guides to go through the mountains. Ask students to read the passage independently and to look at you when they are finished.

Test Items

Distribute the test pages. Remind students that they will want to look back at the passage for help in answering questions.

Say *Point to test item 1. When I read this question, try to make a connection to your own life to help you find the best answer: Which person acts most like Clouds Dancing? Bubble in the choice that tells what person acts most like Clouds Dancing. Wait for students to bubble in their choice. Tell students to look at you when they are finished.*

Tell students to complete the rest of the test by themselves.

Beginning   p. 116

Remind students that this is a test. Tell them that they will complete one test item and that you will read directions for the question. Distribute test page 116. Point to the graphic organizer. Explain that Katrina, a fifth-grader, filled in this chart before writing a report about the lives of the pioneers.

Test Item 1

Point to the first box and point out that the label above it says *Main Idea*. Read the main idea: *The early pioneers had to depend on themselves for everything.* Point to the Cause box and say *They lived far from towns.* Point out that the three boxes next to the Cause box on the left say *Effect*. Point to the first box and say *Pioneers had to grow their own food.* Point to the next box and say *Pioneers had to build their own homes.* Point to empty box 1 at the end of the organizer. Say *One picture is missing. It is the picture that shows what the pioneers did to keep busy at home.* Point to test item 1. Say *Bubble in the choice for the picture that best fits in box 1.* Wait for students to bubble in their choice. Tell students to look at you when they are finished.

Intermediate/Advanced   pp. 116–117

Remind students that this is a test. Tell them that they will complete one test item at a time and that you will read directions for each question. Distribute the test pages. Point to the graphic organizer. Explain that Katrina filled in this chart before writing the paragraph on the lives of the pioneers on page 117. Tell them that they will want to use the graphic organizer page and the paragraph that Katrina wrote to answer the questions on both pages.

Test Item 1

Tell students to read the graphic organizer. Point out the missing picture in the graphic organizer. Point to test item 1. Say *Bubble in the choice for the picture that best fits in box 1.* Wait for students to bubble in their choice. Tell students to look at you when they are finished.

Test Item 2

Point to the blank line (2) and say *Write the sentence that tells what the conclusion is.* Wait for students to write their answer. Tell students to look at you when they are finished.

Tell students that they are going to read the paragraph that Katrina wrote after filling in the chart on page 116. Point to the missing sentences in the writing sample and say *There are two sentences missing.* Tell students to read the paragraph to see what is missing. Wait for students to read the writing sample. Tell students to look at you when they are finished. Remind students to use both the graphic organizer and the writing sample to answer test items 3, 4, and 5.

Test Item 3

Point to test item 3 and say *Read the question and bubble in the choice for blank three.* Wait for students to mark their answers. Tell students to look at you when they are finished.

Test Item 4

Point to test item 4 and say *Read the question and bubble in the choice for blank four.* Wait for students to mark their answers. Tell students to look at you when they are finished.

Test Item 5

Point to test item 5 and say *Read the question and bubble in the best answer choice.* Wait for students to mark their answers. Tell students to look at you when they are finished.

Test Item 6

Point to the sentences in the box at the bottom of the page. Say *Katrina's friend, Angelique, wrote these sentences for her report.* Say *One of Angelique's sentences has a mistake.* Ask students to help fix Angelique's sentence. Say *Find the mistake and bubble in the choice for the sentence that would correct it.* Wait for students to mark their answers. Tell students to look at you when they are finished.

Unit 5 A Growing Nation

Vocabulary Ⓑ

Name _____ Date _____

Directions Look at the pictures. Listen to the question. Bubble in the circle underneath the picture for your answer.

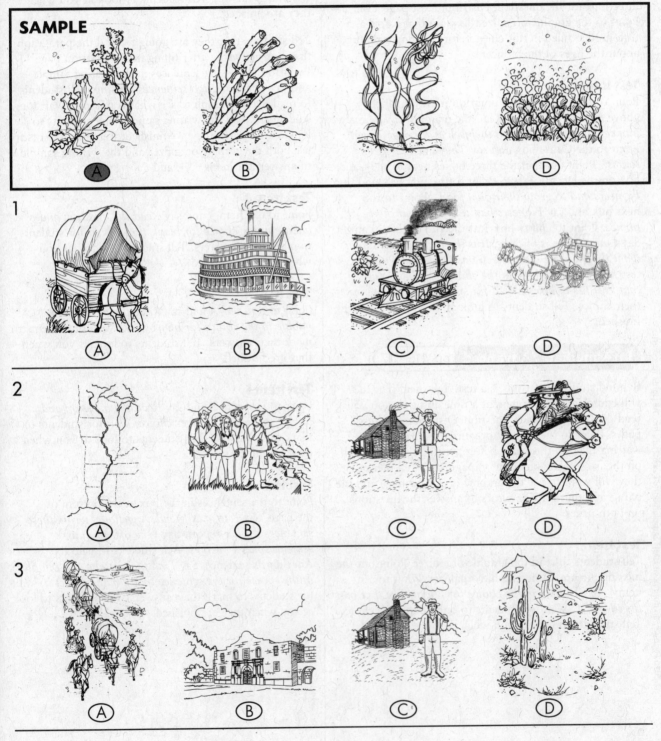

SAMPLE

Ⓐ   Ⓑ   Ⓒ   Ⓓ

1   Ⓐ   Ⓑ   Ⓒ   Ⓓ

2   Ⓐ   Ⓑ   Ⓒ   Ⓓ

3   Ⓐ   Ⓑ   Ⓒ   Ⓓ

Name _____   Date _____

Directions Look at the pictures. Listen to the question. Bubble in the circle underneath the picture for your answer.

SAMPLE

Ⓐ   ⬤Ⓑ

1

Ⓐ   Ⓑ

3

Ⓐ   Ⓑ

2

Ⓐ   Ⓑ

4

Ⓐ   Ⓑ

Name _____ Date _____

© 2010 Rigby®, an imprint of HMH Supplemental Publishers Inc. All rights reserved.

Directions Listen to the selection. Then read each question. Choose the best answer. Bubble in your answer.

A Journey Through the Mountains

1 It is the fall of 1818. Winter is coming.

Mr. Smith's group is near the mountains.

2 Clouds Dancing shows the group a mountain pass.

Mr. Smith is a good leader.

Clouds Dancing is a good guide.

3 It is January in 1819.

They go along the Platte River.

4 The trip is long.

By the spring of 1819, they will be in Oregon.

1 In the sentence *They go along the Platte River,* who are *they*?

mountains   the people in the group   Mr. Smith   trees

Ⓐ   Ⓑ   Ⓒ   Ⓓ

---

2 Clouds Dancing acts most like a _____.

friend   thief   follower   river

Ⓐ   Ⓑ   Ⓒ   Ⓓ

---

3 Mr. Smith is a good leader. Clouds Dancing is a good _____.

mountain   river   guide   group

Ⓐ   Ⓑ   Ⓒ   Ⓓ

---

4 During which season would travel be most difficult?

the summer   the winter   the fall   the spring

Ⓐ   Ⓑ   Ⓒ   Ⓓ

Unit 5   A Growing Nation   Vocabulary ❶

Name _____ Date _____

Directions Read the sentence. Choose the word or
words that best fit in the blank. Bubble in your answer.

SAMPLE

Some reefs in tropical
waters are made
from _____.
- (A) coral
- (B) anglerfish
- (C) bacteria
- (D) salt water

---

3 A person who settled
in the West was known
as a _____.
- (A) pioneer
- (B) frontier
- (C) guide
- (D) hardship

---

1 It was difficult to
_____ the settlers as
they traveled west.
- (A) surround
- (B) survive
- (C) govern
- (D) depend

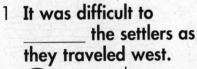

---

4 The movement of people to the West
was called _____.
- (E) frontier
- (F) mission
- (G) westward
  expansion
- (H) wagon

---

2 The _____ rolled
along under the
moonlight.
- (E) hardship
- (F) wagon
- (G) guide
- (H) steamboat

---

5 A Spanish church in the Southwest is
called a _____.
- (A) camp
- (B) stagecoach
- (C) mission
- (D) caravan

Unit 5   A Growing Nation   Grammar ❶

Name _____   Date _____

Directions Read the sentence. Choose the word or words that best fit in the blank. Bubble in your answer.

SAMPLE

The ball is _____.
- (A) bounce
- (B) round
- (C) under
- (D) happily

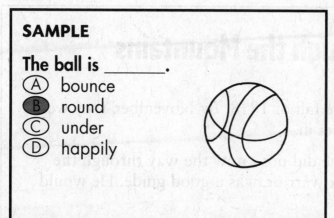

---

1 **Jorge takes a bite of _____ apple.**
- (A) her
- (B) you
- (C) his
- (D) it

2 **It _____ all day yesterday.**
- (E) snows
- (F) have snowing
- (G) was snowing
- (H) to snow

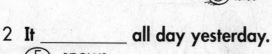

---

3 **The girl _____ a glass of lemonade.**
- (A) to pour
- (B) pouring
- (C) has poured
- (D) have poured

4 **Now we are eating. Earlier, we _____.**
- (E) cooking
- (F) is cooking
- (G) to cook
- (H) were cooking

5 **Luis hit the baseball _____ the fence.**
- (A) on
- (B) under
- (C) in
- (D) over

Unit 5   A Growing Nation

Name _____ Date _____

Directions Read the selection. Then read each question.
Choose the best answer. Bubble in your answer.

Traveling Through the Mountains

Mr. Smith's group left Boston in the fall of 1818. By November, they were near the Plains. Winter was about to set in.

Mr. Smith was a good leader, but he did not know the way through the mountains. Clouds Dancing, the Sioux warrior, was a good guide. He would show the group the way.

During January, 1819, they would go along the Platte River. By spring they would be in Oregon.

1818: *Clouds Dancing shows the group a mountain pass.*

Name _____   Date _____

1 **Which person acts most like Clouds Dancing?**
- Ⓐ an enemy
- Ⓑ a friend
- Ⓒ a child
- Ⓓ a singer

2 **What is the difference between Clouds Dancing and Mr. Smith?**
- Ⓔ Mr. Smith likes the winter, but Clouds Dancing likes the spring.
- Ⓕ Mr. Smith is a good leader, but Clouds Dancing is a good guide.
- Ⓖ Mr. Smith wants to go to Oregon, but Clouds Dancing wants to go East.
- Ⓗ Mr. Smith knows the way through the mountains, but Clouds Dancing does not.

3 *Winter was about to set in.* **What do the words *set in* mean?**
- Ⓐ lead
- Ⓑ start
- Ⓒ know
- Ⓓ good

4 **When the trip started, it was fall. When the trip ended, it was _____.**
- Ⓔ winter
- Ⓕ September
- Ⓖ January
- Ⓗ spring

5 **In the sentence *By November, they were near the Plains,* who are *they*?**
- Ⓐ Mr. Smith's group
- Ⓑ Clouds Dancing
- Ⓒ Mr. Smith and Clouds Dancing
- Ⓓ the mountains

6 **If you were in Mr. Smith's group, why might you want to take the mountain pass?**
- Ⓔ to save time
- Ⓕ to get lost
- Ⓖ to find gold
- Ⓗ to stay warm

Unit 5   A Growing Nation

Vocabulary Ⓐ

Name _____ Date _____

Directions Read the sentence. Choose the word or words that best fit in the blank. Bubble in your answer.

SAMPLE

Some reefs in tropical waters are made from _____.
- Ⓐ coral
- Ⓑ anglerfish
- Ⓒ bacteria
- Ⓓ salt water

---

1 It was difficult to _____ the settlers as they traveled west.
- Ⓐ surround
- Ⓑ survive
- Ⓒ govern
- Ⓓ depend

2 The _____ rolled along under the moonlight.
- Ⓔ hardship
- Ⓕ wagon
- Ⓖ guide
- Ⓗ steamboat

3 A person who settled in the West was known as a _____.
- Ⓐ pioneer
- Ⓑ frontier
- Ⓒ guide
- Ⓓ hardship

4 The movement of people to the West was called _____.
- Ⓔ frontier
- Ⓕ mission
- Ⓖ westward expansion
- Ⓗ wagon

5 A Spanish church in the Southwest is called a _____.
- Ⓐ camp
- Ⓑ stagecoach
- Ⓒ mission
- Ⓓ caravan

Unit 5   A Growing Nation

Grammar Ⓐ

Name _____   Date _____

Directions Read the sentence. Choose the word or words that best fit in the blank. Bubble in your answer.

SAMPLE

The ball is _____.
- Ⓐ bounce
- ● round
- Ⓒ under
- Ⓓ happily

---

1 Jorge takes a bite of _____ apple.
- Ⓐ her
- Ⓑ you
- Ⓒ his
- Ⓓ it

2 It _____ all day yesterday.
- Ⓔ snows
- Ⓕ have snowing
- Ⓖ was snowing
- Ⓗ to snow

3 The girl _____ a glass of lemonade.
- Ⓐ to pour
- Ⓑ pouring
- Ⓒ has poured
- Ⓓ have poured

4 Now we are eating. Earlier, we _____.
- Ⓔ cooking
- Ⓕ is cooking
- Ⓖ to cook
- Ⓗ were cooking

5 Luis hit the baseball _____ the fence.
- Ⓐ on
- Ⓑ under
- Ⓒ in
- Ⓓ over

Name _____ Date _____

Directions Read the selection. Then read each question.
Choose the best answer. Bubble in your answer.

A Journey Through the Mountains

Mr. Smith's group left Boston, Massachusetts, in the fall of 1818.
Now it was November 1818. Winter was about to set in.

Mr. Smith was a good leader, but he did not know the challenges of
the Plains or the passages through the mountains. So Mr. Smith asked
the Sioux warrior, Clouds Dancing, to guide the group.

1818: *Clouds Dancing shows the group a mountain pass.*

Name _____ Date _____

Clouds Dancing approached the wagon. The Sioux and the pioneers both liked to trade goods. Clouds Dancing traded his moccasins for pretty beads.

He was excited. The trip would be difficult, but they would succeed.

During January, 1819, they traveled along the Platte River. By the spring of 1819, Clouds Dancing guided them to Oregon.

Name _____   Date _____

1 **Which person acts most like Clouds Dancing?**
   Ⓐ an enemy
   Ⓑ a friend
   Ⓒ a child
   Ⓓ a singer

2 **What is the difference between Clouds Dancing and Mr. Smith?**
   Ⓔ Mr. Smith likes the winter, but Clouds Dancing likes the spring.
   Ⓕ Mr. Smith is a good leader, but Clouds Dancing is a good guide.
   Ⓖ Mr. Smith wants to go to Oregon, but Clouds Dancing wants to go to Boston.
   Ⓗ Mr. Smith knows the way through the mountains, but Clouds Dancing does not.

3 *Winter was about to set in.* **What do the words *set in* mean?**
   Ⓐ lead
   Ⓑ start
   Ⓒ know
   Ⓓ good

4 **When the trip started, it was fall. When the trip ended, it was _____.**
   Ⓔ winter
   Ⓕ September
   Ⓖ January
   Ⓗ spring

5 **In the sentence *By November, they were near the Plains,* who are *they*?**
   Ⓐ Mr. Smith's group
   Ⓑ Clouds Dancing
   Ⓒ Mr. Smith and Clouds Dancing
   Ⓓ the mountains

6 **If you were in Mr. Smith's group, why might you want to take the mountain pass?**
   Ⓔ to save time
   Ⓕ to get lost
   Ⓖ to find gold
   Ⓗ to stay warm

Writing

Writing ⒷⒾⒶ

Name _____   Date _____

Directions Look at the graphic organizer and student writing sample on page 117. Then answer the questions.

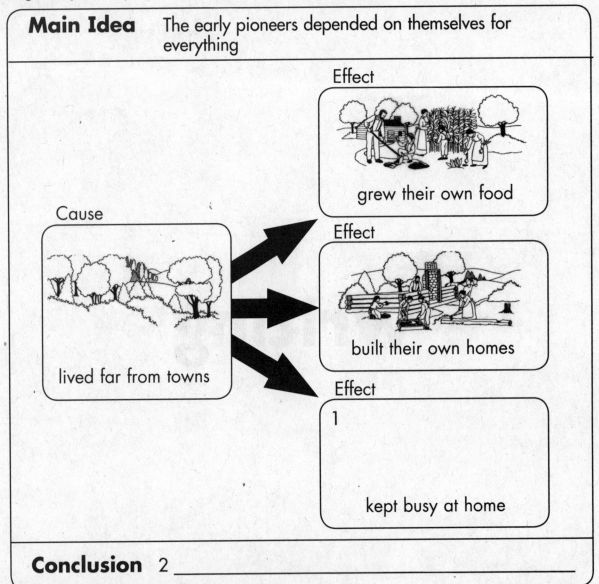

Main Idea   The early pioneers depended on themselves for everything

Effect: grew their own food

Cause: lived far from towns

Effect: built their own homes

Effect: 1 kept busy at home

Conclusion 2 _____

---

1 **Which picture best fits in box 1?**

Ⓐ

Ⓑ

2 **Fill in blank 2.**

Name _____   Date _____

The early pioneers had to depend on themselves for everything. They lived far from towns. (3) _____. There were no stores in which to buy food. (4) _____. They kept busy in the house, too. Life in the new frontier was difficult.

---

3 **Which sentence best fits blank 3?**
  Ⓐ They were sad.
  Ⓑ They had to grow their own food.
  Ⓒ They liked living far away from everyone.

4 **Which sentence best fits blank 4?**
  Ⓐ They liked to watch movies.
  Ⓑ They went on many trips for fun.
  Ⓒ They built their own homes.

5 **Which sentence in the report above has a detail about pioneer life?**
  Ⓐ The early pioneers had to depend on themselves for everything.
  Ⓑ There were no stores in which to buy food.
  Ⓒ Life in the new frontier was difficult.

The pioneers worked hard. They had chop their own wood.

---

6 **What would make the second sentence in the box above correct?**
  Ⓐ They has chopped their own wood.
  Ⓑ They had chopping their own wood.
  Ⓒ They had to chop their own wood.

Beginning

Student _____   Teacher _____

Test Section	Skills Tested	Item Number	Total Scores	Reteaching Tools (For additional reteaching activities, see p. T14)
VOCABULARY *Date Tested:* _____	Words related to the settlement of the American West	1, 2, 3	□ × 9 points = /27	Newcomer Book Academic Language Builder Song Charts Chant Posters Language Practice Game Concept Posters TPR Cards Audio CDs

GRAMMAR
 	
Date Tested:
_____
	Prepositions: *in, under*
	
	Pronouns: *her, they*
		1, 3
		
		2, 4
			□
			×
			8 points
			=
			/32
				Prepositions:
				  Teacher's Guide p. 248
				
				Pronouns:
				  Teacher's Guide p. 258

READING
 	
Date Tested:
_____
	Word Study: Pronouns
	Comprehension Strategy:
	  Make Connections
	Literary Analysis:
	  Compare and Contrast Characters
		1
		2, 4
		
		3
			□
			×
			8 points
			=
			/32
				Word Study:
				  Teacher's Guide p. 263
				
				Comprehension Strategy:
				  Teacher's Guide p. 257
				
				Literary Analysis:
				  Teacher's Guide pp. 263

WRITING *Date Tested:* _____	**Writing Form:** Report	1	□ × 9 points = /9	**Writing Form:** Teacher's Guide pp. 247, 249, 251, 253, 257, 259, 261

SKILLS TO BE DEVELOPED	UNIT 5 **Total Score** /100	COMMENTS
RETEACHING GROUP ASSIGNMENT		

| **WRITING COMPOSITION EVALUATION**

Date Tested:
_____ | Obtain individual student writing sample — Teacher's Guide, Week 4 Lesson 4, p. 287 | Figure score using pp. A14–A16

Composite Score □ | See appropriate mini-lessons in the *Writing Resource Guide* and Shared Writing lessons in the Teacher's Guide, pp. 247, 249, 251, 253, 257, 259, 261 |

Student Profile | Unit 5 Progress Test

Intermediate/Advanced

Student _____

Teacher _____

Test Section	Skills Tested	Item Number	Total Scores	Reteaching Tools (For additional reteaching activities, see p. T14)
VOCABULARY *Date Tested:* _____	Words related to the settlement of the American West	1, 2, 3, 4, 5	☐ x 4 points = /20	Newcomer Book Academic Language Builder Song Charts Chant Posters Language Practice Game Concept Posters TPR Cards Audio CDs
GRAMMAR *Date Tested:* _____	Pronoun: *his* Past Continuous Present Perfect Preposition: *over*	1 2, 4 3 5	☐ x 4 points = /20	**Pronouns:** Teacher's Guide p. 258 **Past Continuous:** Teacher's Guide p. 246 **Present Perfect:** Teacher's Guide p. 284 **Prepositions:** Teacher's Guide p. 248
READING *Date Tested:* _____	**Comprehension Strategy:** Make Connections **Literary Analysis:** Compare and Contrast Characters, Settings **Word Study:** Idioms; Pronouns	1, 6 2, 4 3, 5	☐ x 5 points = /30	**Comprehension Strategy:** Teacher's Guide p. 257 **Literary Analysis:** Teacher's Guide p. 263 **Word Study:** Teacher's Guide pp. 281, 263
WRITING *Date Tested:* _____	**Writing Form:** Report **Written Convention:** Infinitives	1, 2 3, 4, 5 6	☐ x 5 points = /30	**Writing Form:** Teacher's Guide pp. 247, 249, 251, 253, 257, 259, 261 **Written Convention:** Teacher's Guide p. 261
SKILLS TO BE DEVELOPED **RETEACHING GROUP ASSIGNMENT**		**UNIT 5** **Total Score** /100		**COMMENTS**
WRITING COMPOSITION EVALUATION *Date Tested:* _____	Obtain individual student writing sample — Teacher's Guide, Week 4 Lesson 4, p. 287	Figure score using pp. A14–A16 **Composite Score** ☐		See appropriate mini-lessons in the *Writing Resource Guide* and Shared Writing lessons in the Teacher's Guide, pp. 247, 249, 251, 253, 257, 259, 261

Name _____   Date _____

Things I Know About Reading in English!

When I read, I think about what I already know in English.

Yes   **Sometimes**   **Not Yet**

I can compare and contrast characters in a story.

Yes   **Sometimes**   **Not Yet**

Texts I Can Read in English!

The Nez Perce Help Us!

Journey on the Royal Road

_____

My Goals:

_____

_____

_____

Things I Can Say in English!

I can talk about early times in North America.

Yes   **Sometimes**   **Not Yet**

I can use pronouns instead of names in English.

Yes   **Sometimes**   **Not Yet**

My Goals:

_____

_____

_____

Things I Know About Writing in English!

I can use a graphic organizer to plan my report.

Yes   **Sometimes**   **Not Yet**

My Goals:

_____

_____

_____

Unit 6
Progress Test

Beginning p. 126

Remind students that this is a test. Tell them that they will complete one test item at a time and that you will read directions for each question.

Sample

Distribute the test page. Point to the sample box. Tell students to look at the pictures in the box as you say and point to each picture: *This picture shows the Mississippi River. This picture shows a railroad. This picture shows a wagon. This picture shows a steamboat.* Ask *Which picture shows a wagon?* Wait for students to respond orally. Say *Bubble C is filled in because we were looking for a wagon.*

Test Items

Say the following directions for each test item. Then wait for students to bubble in their choice. Tell students to look at you when they are finished with each item.

1. Have students point to item number 1 and say *Look at the pictures in row one. Which picture shows a satellite?* Tell students to bubble in the circle under the picture that shows a *satellite*.

2. Have students point to item number 2 and say *Look at the pictures in row two. Which picture shows a patent?* Tell students to bubble in the circle under the picture that shows a *patent*.

3. Have students point to item number 3 and say *Look at the pictures in row three. Which picture shows communicate?* Tell students to bubble in the circle under the picture that shows *communicate*.

Intermediate p. 130 **Advanced** p. 134

Remind students that this is a test. Tell them that they will complete one test item at a time and that you will read directions for each question.

Sample

Distribute the test page. Point to the sample sentence in the box. Tell students that one or more words are missing in the sentence. Say *Read this sentence with me. Each* blank *rolled across the prairie.* Say *Now we will read the sentence again with each answer choice to see which one best fits in the blank. Each* railroad *rolled across the prairie. Each* steamboat *rolled across the prairie. Each* wagon *rolled across the prairie. Each* Mississippi River *rolled across the prairie.* Ask *Which word or words would make sense to put in the blank?* Wait for students to respond orally. Tell students that bubble C is filled in because *Each wagon rolled across the prairie* is the correct choice.

Test Items

Say the following directions for each test item. Then wait for students to bubble in their choice. Tell students to look at you when they are finished with each item.

1. Say *Point to test item 1. Read the sentence with me. George got a* blank *from the government for his invention.* Then say *Read the sentence again and try each word in the blank.*

   Wait for students to read, then say *Bubble in the choice for the word that goes in the blank.*

2. Say *Point to test item 2. Read the sentence with me. Milly's father builds* blank *to put into space.* Then say *Read the sentence again and try each word in the blank.*

   Wait for students to read, then say *Bubble in the choice for the word that goes in the blank.*

3. Say *Point to test item 3. Read the sentence with me. The* blank *helped people send messages in the 1800's.* Then say *Read the sentence again and try each word in the blank.*

   Wait for students to read, then say *Bubble in the choice for the word that goes in the blank.*

4. Say *Point to test item 4. Read the sentences with me. We can talk to each other on the telephone. Talking is how we* blank. Then say *Read the sentences again and try each word in the blank.*

   Wait for students to read, then say *Bubble in the choice for the word that goes in the blank.*

5. Say *Point to test item 5. Read the sentence with me. Science has helped* blank *the way we travel.* Then say *Read the sentence again and try each word in the blank.*

   Wait for students to read, then say *Bubble in the choice for the word that goes in the blank.*

Teacher Directions | Unit 6 Progress Test

Grammar

Technology Matters!

Beginning — p. 127

Remind students that this is a test. Tell them that they will complete one test item at a time and that you will read directions for each question.

Sample

Distribute the test page. Point to the sample box. Tell students to look at the pictures in the box as you say and point to each picture: *This picture shows* Mr. Ortiz is in his truck. *This picture shows* Mr. Ortiz is outside his truck. *Which picture shows* Mr. Ortiz is in his truck? Wait for students to respond orally. Then say *Bubble* A *is filled in because we were looking for* Mr. Ortiz is in his truck.

Test Items

Say the following directions for each test item. Then wait for students to bubble in their choice. Tell students to look at you when they are finished with each item.

1. Have students point to item number 1 and say *Look at the pictures. Listen. Which picture shows* Pierre moves quickly?

   Tell students to bubble in the circle under the picture that shows *Pierre moves quickly.*

2. Have students point to item number 2 and say *Look at the pictures. Listen. Which picture shows* Rosita likes this pencil?

   Tell students to bubble in the circle under the picture that shows *Rosita likes this pencil.*

3. Have students point to item number 3 and say *Look at the pictures. Listen. Which picture shows* Someday Kee will ride on a maglev train?

   Tell students to bubble in the circle under the picture that shows *Someday Kee will ride on a maglev train.*

4. Have students point to item number 4 and say *Look at the pictures. Listen. Which picture shows* She is going to wake up soon?

   Tell students to bubble in the circle under the picture that shows *She is going to wake up soon.*

Intermediate — p. 131   Advanced — p. 135

Remind students that this is a test. Tell them that they will complete one test item at a time and that you will read directions for each question.

Sample

Distribute the test page. Point to the sample sentence in the box. Tell students that one or more words are missing in the sentence. Say *Read this sentence with me.* Jorge blank *a bite of his apple.* Say *Now we will read the sentence again with each choice to see which one best fits in the blank.* Jorge to take *a bite of his apple.* Jorge has taken *a bite of his apple.* Jorge have taken *a bite of his apple.* Jorge taking *a bite of his apple.* Ask *Which word or words would make sense to put in the blank?* Wait for students to respond orally. Tell students that bubble *B* is filled in because *Jorge has taken a bite of his apple* is the correct choice.

Test Items

Say the following directions for each test item. Then wait for students to bubble in their choice. Tell students to look at you when they are finished with each item.

1. Say *Point to test item 1. Read the sentence with me. The people wave to* blank *plane in the sky.* Then say *Read the sentence and try each word in the blank.*

   Wait for students to read, then say *Bubble in the choice for the answer that goes in the blank.*

2. Say *Point to test item 2. Read the sentence with me. We* blank *have dinner soon.* Then say *Read the sentence and try each word in the blank.*

   Wait for students to read, then say *Bubble in the choice for the answer that goes in the blank.*

3. Say *Point to test item 3. Read the sentence with me. We are* blank *sing and dance.* Then say *Read the sentence and try each answer in the blank.*

   Wait for students to read, then say *Bubble in the choice for the answer that goes in the blank.*

4. Say *Point to test item 4. Read the sentence with me. We* wash *blank* soap. Then say *Read the sentence and try each word in the blank.*

   Wait for students to read, then say *Bubble in the choice for the answer that goes in the blank.*

5. Say *Point to test item 5. Read the sentence with me. The clock is ticking* blank. Then say *Read the sentence and try each word in the blank.*

   Wait for students to read, then say *Bubble in the choice for the answer that goes in the blank.*

Reading

Technology Matters!

© 2010 Rigby®, an imprint of HMH Supplemental Publishers Inc. All rights reserved.

Beginning pp. 128–129

Remind students that this is a test. Tell them that they will complete one test item at a time and that you will read directions for each question.

Passage

Distribute the reading passage on page 128. Have students point to the pictures in the boxes. Explain that this is a true story about a famous inventor. Ask students to follow along as you read the passage aloud. Point to each illustration as you read the corresponding text.

Say *Listen as I read* **"The Plant Man."**

1. *Look at picture 1.*   *George Washington Carver was an inventor.*
   He studied farming.

2. *Look at picture 2.*   *He experimented with sweet potatoes.*
   He tried using sweet potatoes to make other things. It worked!

3. *Look at picture 3.*   *This helped farmers sell their sweet potatoes.*

   Say *Point to the list in box 3. Read the list with me. Things Made from Sweet Potatoes: writing ink, paper, paint, library paste, flour*

4. *Look at picture 4.*   *He was good at finding different ways to use plants.*
   He was a smart man.

Test Items

Distribute test page 129. Say the following directions for each test item. Read aloud the question. Give students time to read and look at the pictures. Then wait for students to bubble in their choice. Tell students to look at you when they are finished with each item.

1. Say *Point to test item 1. Look at the pictures. Read the question with me. Look at the story. Who is the story about? Bubble in the choice that shows who the story is about.*

2. Say *Point to test item 2. Read the question with me. Mr. Carver helped farmers. Which word best describes Mr. Carver? Bubble in the choice for the word that tells that Mr. Carver helped.*

3. Say *Point to test item 3. Read the question with me. Which picture shows you what an inventor does? Use pictures from the story to help you figure out what an inventor does. Bubble in the choice that tells what an inventor does.*

4. Say *Point to test item 4. What does the word* experimented *mean? Use context in the story to help you figure out what the word experimented means. Bubble in your answer choice.*

Intermediate pp. 132–133
Advanced pp. 136–138

Remind students that this is a test. Explain that they will read the passage on their own and complete the test items.

Passage

Distribute the reading passages. Have students point to the passage. Point to the graphic in the passage. Explain that graphic information goes with the passage and that they will read this as well as the passage. Tell students they are going to read about a famous inventor. Ask students to read the passage independently and to look at you when they are finished.

Test Items

Distribute the test pages. Remind students that they will want to look back at the passage for help in answering questions.

Say *Point to test item 1. Read the question with me. George Washington Carver helped farmers make more money* blank *sweet potatoes. Read and bubble in the choice that has the correct preposition.* Wait for students to bubble in their choice. Tell students to look at you when they are finished.

Tell students to complete the rest of the test themselves.

Teacher Directions | Unit 6 Progress Test

Writing

Technology Matters!

Beginning p. 140

Remind students that this is a test. Tell them that they will complete one test item and that you will read directions for the question. Distribute test page 140. Point to the graphic organizer. Explain that Daniel, a fifth-grade student, filled in this chart before writing about using a computer to write a report.

Test Item 1

Tell students this group is using a computer to do a report. Point to the first picture and say *This group is using the Internet to get information.* Point to the picture at the bottom and say *This student has written his report on the computer. Now he is using the spellchecker on the computer to help him fix his spelling.* Point to empty box 1 in the middle. Say *One picture is missing. It is a picture that shows how a student put pictures into her report.* Point to test item 1. Say *Bubble in the choice for the picture that best fits in box 1.* Wait for students to bubble in their choice. Tell students to look at you when they are finished.

Intermediate/Advanced pp. 140–141

Remind students that this is a test. Tell them that they will complete one test item at a time and that you will read directions for each question. Distribute the test pages. Point to the graphic organizer. Explain that Daniel, a fifth-grade student, filled in this chart before writing the paragraph about how his group used a computer to write a report. Tell students that they will want to use the graphic organizer page and the paragraph that Daniel wrote to answer the questions on both pages.

Test Item 1

Tell students to read the graphic organizer. Point out the missing picture in the graphic organizer. Point to test item 1. Say *Bubble in the choice for the picture that best fits in box 1.* Wait for students to bubble in their choice. Tell students to look at you when they are finished.

Test Item 2

Point to the blank line (2) and say *Label the picture telling what the students did.* Wait for students to write their answer. Tell students to look at you when they are finished.

Tell students that they are going to read the paragraph that Daniel wrote after filling in the chart on page 140. Point to the missing sentences in the writing sample and say *There are two sentences missing.* Tell students to read the paragraph to see what is missing. Wait for students to read the writing sample. Tell students to look at you when they are finished. Remind students to use both the graphic organizer and the paragraph to answer test items 3, 4, and 5.

Test Item 3

Point to test item 3 and say *Read the question and bubble in the choice for blank three.* Wait for students to bubble in their answers. Tell students to look at you when they are finished.

Test Item 4

Point to test item 4 and say *Read the question and bubble in the choice for blank four.* Wait for students to bubble in their answers. Tell students to look at you when they are finished.

Test Item 5

Point to test item 5 and say *Read the question and bubble in your choice.* Wait for students to bubble in their answers. Tell students to look at you when they are finished.

Test Item 6

Point to the sentences in the box at the bottom of the page. Say *Daniel's friend, Becky, wrote these sentences about using the computer.* Say *One of Becky's sentences has a mistake.* Ask students to fix Becky's sentence. Say *Find the mistake and bubble in the choice for the sentence that would correct it.* Wait for students to bubble in their answers. Tell students to look at you when they are finished.

Name _____   Date _____

Directions Look at the pictures. Listen to the question.
Bubble in the circle underneath the picture for your answer.

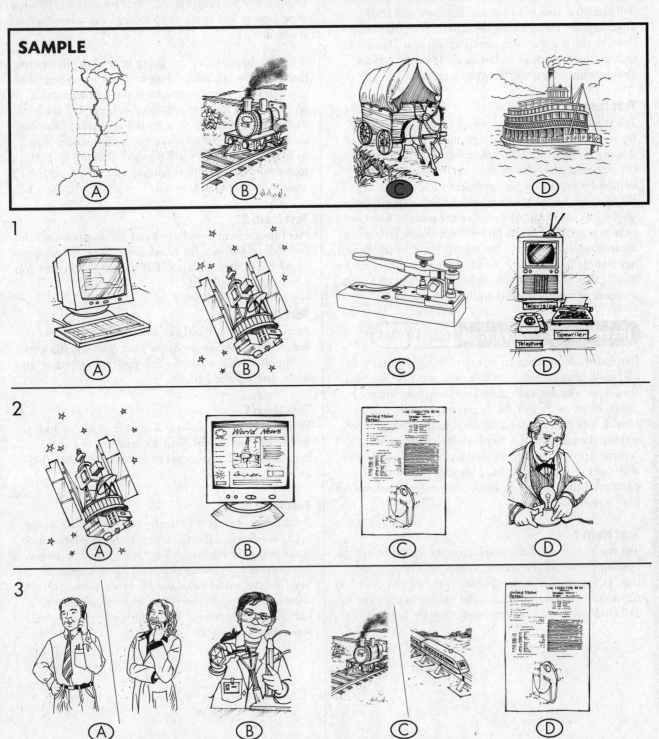

SAMPLE

Ⓐ   Ⓑ   Ⓒ   Ⓓ

1   Ⓐ   Ⓑ   Ⓒ   Ⓓ

2   Ⓐ   Ⓑ   Ⓒ   Ⓓ

3   Ⓐ   Ⓑ   Ⓒ   Ⓓ

Unit 6   Technology Matters!   Grammar Ⓑ

Name _____   Date _____

Directions Look at the pictures. Listen to the question.
Bubble in the circle underneath the picture for your answer.

SAMPLE

Ⓐ   Ⓑ

1

Ⓐ   Ⓑ

3

Ⓐ

Ⓑ

2

Ⓐ   Ⓑ

4

Ⓐ   Ⓑ

Name _____ Date _____

Directions Listen to the selection. Then read each question.
Choose the best answer. Bubble in your answer.

The Plant Man

1 George Washington Carver was an inventor.

He studied farming.

2 He experimented with sweet potatoes.

He tried using sweet potatoes to make other things. It worked!

3 This helped farmers sell their sweet potatoes.

4 He was good at finding different ways to use plants.

He was a smart man.

Things Made from Sweet Potatoes
- writing ink
- paper
- paint
- library paste
- flour

Name _____ Date _____

1 Look at the story. Who is the story about?

sweet potato
Ⓐ

paint
Ⓑ

farmer
Ⓒ

George Washington
Carver
Ⓓ

---

2 Mr. Carver helped farmers. Which word best describes Mr. Carver?

helpful
Ⓐ

helpless
Ⓑ

careful
Ⓒ

awful
Ⓓ

---

3 Which picture shows you what an inventor does?

He likes plants.
Ⓐ

He is a farmer.
Ⓑ

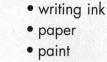

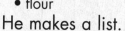
• writing ink
• paper
• paint
• library paste
• flour
He makes a list.
Ⓒ

He experiments.
Ⓓ

---

4 What does the word *experimented* mean?

farmed
Ⓐ

tried to
do something
Ⓑ

looked at leaves
Ⓒ

put on an apron
Ⓓ

Unit 6 Technology Matters!   Vocabulary ❶

Name _____   Date _____

Directions Read the sentences. Choose the word that best fits in the blank. Bubble in your answer.

SAMPLE

Each _____ rolled across the prairie.

- (A) railroad
- (B) steamboat
- (C) wagon
- (D) Mississippi River

---

1 George got a _____ from the government for his invention.

- (A) patent
- (B) telegraph
- (C) satellite
- (D) device

2 Milly's father builds _____ to put into space.

- (E) labor
- (F) satellites
- (G) patents
- (H) telegraphs

3 The _____ helped people send messages in the 1800's.

- (A) satellite
- (B) model
- (C) patent
- (D) telegraph

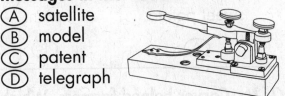

4 We can talk to each other on the telephone. Talking is how we
_____.

- (E) impact
- (F) develop
- (G) communicate
- (H) improve

5 Science has helped _____ the way we travel.

- (A) communicate
- (B) patent
- (C) improve
- (D) transportation

Name _____ Date _____

Directions Read the sentence. Choose the word that best fits in the blank. Bubble in your answer.

SAMPLE

Jorge _____ a bite of his apple.
- Ⓐ to take
- 🅱 has taken
- Ⓒ have taken
- Ⓓ taking

---

1 The people wave to _____ plane in the sky.
- Ⓐ these
- Ⓑ those
- Ⓒ that
- Ⓓ then

2 We _____ have dinner soon.
- Ⓔ will
- Ⓕ are
- Ⓖ is
- Ⓗ to

---

3 We are _____ sing and dance.
- Ⓐ will
- Ⓑ going
- Ⓒ is
- Ⓓ going to

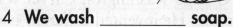

4 We wash _____ soap.
- Ⓔ on
- Ⓕ in
- Ⓖ with
- Ⓗ above

5 The clock is ticking _____.
- Ⓐ quietly
- Ⓑ quiet
- Ⓒ quiteness
- Ⓓ quieted

Name _____   Date _____

Directions Read the selection. Then read each
question. Choose the best answer. Bubble in your answer.

The Amazing Plant Man

George Washington Carver was an amazing inventor. He studied
farming. He invented different uses for plants to help farmers make
money. He experimented mostly with peanuts, but he also tried
making things from sweet potatoes. From sweet potatoes he made
writing ink, paint, and flour. People could use sweet potatoes in more
ways, so they bought more sweet potatoes from the farmers. The
farmers were able to make more money. George Washington Carver
became famous throughout the world.

Things Made from Sweet Potatoes
- writing ink
- paper
- paint
- library paste
- flour

Unit 7   Earth, Moon, and Sun   Grammar Ⓑ

Name _____   Date _____

Directions Look at the pictures. Listen to the question.
Bubble in the circle underneath the picture for your answer.

SAMPLE

Ⓐ   🅑

1

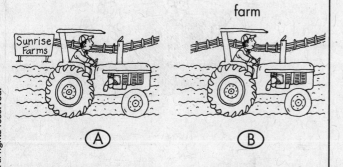

Sunrise Farms   farm

Ⓐ   Ⓑ

3

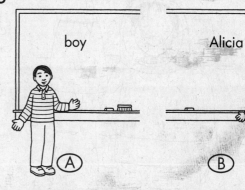

boy   Alicia

Ⓐ   Ⓑ

2

Earth   planets

Ⓐ   Ⓑ

4

Mae Jemison   astronaut

Ⓐ   Ⓑ

Name _____   Date _____

Directions   Listen to the selection. Then read each question. Choose the best answer. Bubble in your answer.

Living on Mars

1 My name is Pele. I am a student on Mars.

It took me six months to fly here.

2 There are volcanic craters on Mars.

I play crater hockey. Yesterday, my team beat the Martians.

3 I wear special clothes because Mars is like an ice ball.

The average temperature is −73.4° Fahrenheit, but my clothes keep me warm.

4 Living on Mars is like living in a deep freezer.

Name _____   Date _____

1 *It took me six months to fly here.* **What does this sentence help you understand about Mars?**

Mars has volcanic craters.	Mars is very far from Earth.	They play hockey on Mars.	Special clothes are needed on Mars.
Ⓐ	Ⓑ	Ⓒ	Ⓓ

2 Which event seems real?

playing crater hockey	living on Mars	being a student on Mars	wearing special clothes for the cold
Ⓐ	Ⓑ	Ⓒ	Ⓓ

3 Which sentence has a conjunction?

My name is pele	There are volcanic craters.	I play crater hockey.	The average temperature is −73.4 °F., but my clothes keep me warm.
Ⓐ	Ⓑ	Ⓒ	Ⓓ

-73.4°F

4 Pele says that _____ is like an ice ball.

Mars	a crater	hockey	a Martian
Ⓐ	Ⓑ	Ⓒ	Ⓓ

Unit 7 Earth, Moon, and Sun   Vocabulary ❶

Name _____ Date _____

Directions Read the sentence. Choose the word or words that best fit in the blank. Bubble in your answer.

SAMPLE

_____ are in space.
- Ⓐ Telegraphs
- ⬤Ⓑ Satellites
- Ⓒ Patents
- Ⓓ Models

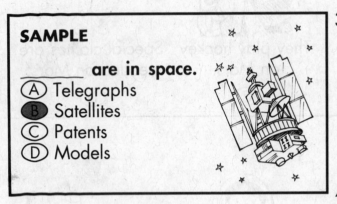

1 **We use a _____ to see planets.**
- Ⓐ telescope
- Ⓑ rover
- Ⓒ crater
- Ⓓ space station

2 **The _____ is like a car. It goes on the surface of Mars or the moon.**

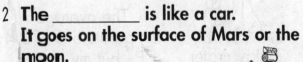
- Ⓔ equipment
- Ⓕ rover
- Ⓖ space station
- Ⓗ spacecraft

3 **Astronauts can live on a _____.**
- Ⓐ space station
- Ⓑ rover
- Ⓒ axis
- Ⓓ outer planet

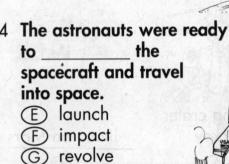

4 **The astronauts were ready to _____ the spacecraft and travel into space.**
- Ⓔ launch
- Ⓕ impact
- Ⓖ revolve
- Ⓗ develop

5 **A hole on the surface of the moon is called a _____. Some are as big as football fields.**
- Ⓐ flight
- Ⓑ crater
- Ⓒ distance
- Ⓓ lunar

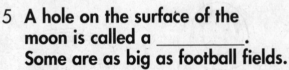

Name _____ Date _____

Directions Read the sentence. Choose the word that best fits in the blank. Bubble in your answer.

SAMPLE

We wash _____ soap.
- Ⓐ on
- Ⓑ at
- ⬤ with
- Ⓓ above

1 A cow _____ flies.
- Ⓐ always
- Ⓑ never
- Ⓒ often
- Ⓓ sometimes

2 Susita feels hot _____ the sun is shining.
- Ⓔ because
- Ⓕ from
- Ⓖ and
- Ⓗ but

3 The name of the student is _____.
- Ⓐ girl
- Ⓑ woman
- Ⓒ Angie
- Ⓓ teacher

4 The moon is big, but Earth is _____.
- Ⓔ bigger
- Ⓕ big
- Ⓖ biggest
- Ⓗ small

5 I like the new glove _____ I got for my birthday.
- Ⓐ but
- Ⓑ and
- Ⓒ because
- Ⓓ that

Name _____ Date _____

Directions Read the selection. Then read each question. Choose the best answer. Bubble in your answer.

My Life on Mars

My name is Pele. I am an exchange student on Mars. It took six months to fly here. I live with a Martian family.

Living on Mars is like living in a deep freezer. I wear special clothes because Mars is like an ice ball. The average temperature is –73.4° Fahrenheit, but my clothes keep me warm. It's too cold to grow plants on Mars.

There are volcanic craters. I play crater hockey. Yesterday, my team beat the Martians.

Name _____ Date _____

1 *It took six months to fly here.*
**What does this sentence help you
understand about Mars?**
- Ⓐ Mars has volcanic craters.
- Ⓑ Mars is very far from Earth.
- Ⓒ They play hockey on Mars.
- Ⓓ Special clothes are needed on
Mars.

2 *I play crater hockey.* **What does this
sentence help you understand about
Pele's life on Mars?**
- Ⓔ He is cold.
- Ⓕ He has fun on Mars.
- Ⓖ He is hungry.
- Ⓗ He doesn't have any friends.

3 **Which event seems real?**
- Ⓐ There are volcanic craters on
Mars.
- Ⓑ Pele goes to school on Mars.
- Ⓒ Pele's team beat the Martians.
- Ⓓ Pele lives with a Martian family.

4 **Which sentence has a conjunction?**
- Ⓔ Mars is like an ice ball.
- Ⓕ Pele plays crater hockey.
- Ⓖ The air on Mars is cold.
- Ⓗ The average temperature is
−73.4° Fahrenheit, but my
clothes keep me warm.

5 **What is the story mostly about?**
- Ⓐ an exchange student's life on
Mars
- Ⓑ how to play crater hockey
- Ⓒ what to wear on Mars
- Ⓓ where to see Martians

6 **Pele thinks living on Mars is like
living _____.**
- Ⓔ with a hockey team
- Ⓕ in a deep freezer
- Ⓖ in a crater
- Ⓗ on Earth

Unit 7 Earth, Moon, and Sun Vocabulary Ⓐ

Name _____ Date _____

Directions Read the sentence. Choose the word or words that best fit in the blank. Bubble in your answer.

SAMPLE

_____ are in space.
- Ⓐ Telegraphs
- Ⓑ Satellites
- Ⓒ Patents
- Ⓓ Models

---

1 We use a _____ to see planets.
- Ⓐ telescope
- Ⓑ rover
- Ⓒ crater
- Ⓓ space station

2 The _____ is like a car. It goes on the surface of Mars or the moon.
- Ⓔ equipment
- Ⓕ rover
- Ⓖ space station
- Ⓗ spacecraft

3 Astronauts can live on a _____.
- Ⓐ space station
- Ⓑ rover
- Ⓒ axis
- Ⓓ outer planet

4 The astronauts were ready to _____ the spacecraft and travel into space.
- Ⓔ launch
- Ⓕ impact
- Ⓖ revolve
- Ⓗ develop

5 A hole on the surface of the moon is called a _____. Some are as big as football fields.
- Ⓐ flight
- Ⓑ crater
- Ⓒ distance
- Ⓓ lunar

Name _____ Date _____

Directions Read the sentence. Choose the word that best fits in the blank. Bubble in your answer.

SAMPLE

We wash _____ soap.
- (A) on
- (B) at
- (C) with
- (D) above

---

1 A cow _____ flies.
- (A) always
- (B) never
- (C) often
- (D) sometimes

2 Susita feels hot _____ the sun is shining.
- (E) because
- (F) from
- (G) and
- (H) but

3 The name of the student is _____.
- (A) girl
- (B) woman
- (C) Angie
- (D) teacher

4 The moon is big, but Earth is _____.
- (E) bigger
- (F) big
- (G) biggest
- (H) small

5 I like the new glove _____ I got for my birthday.
- (A) but
- (B) and
- (C) because
- (D) that

Name _____   Date _____

Directions Read the selection. Then read each question. Choose the best answer. Bubble in your answer.

My Life on Mars

My name is Pele. I am an exchange student on Mars. It took six months to fly here. It is the year 2027, and humans have been on Mars since 2020.

I wear special clothes because Mars is like an ice ball. The average temperature is –73.4° Fahrenheit, but my clothes keep me warm. Living on Mars is like living in a deep freezer.

Name _____ Date _____

The cold air does not allow plants to grow. My Martian family grows plants in specially heated globes.

Seeing who can jump the highest and the farthest is a fun activity. There are volcanic craters, too. I play crater hockey. Yesterday, my team beat the Martians.

Name _____ Date _____

1 *It took six months to fly here.*
   **What does this sentence help you
   understand about Mars?**
   - Ⓐ Mars has volcanic craters.
   - Ⓑ Mars is very far from Earth.
   - Ⓒ They play hockey on Mars.
   - Ⓓ Special clothes are needed on
     Mars.

2 *I play crater hockey.* **What does this
   sentence help you understand about
   Pele's life on Mars?**
   - Ⓔ He is cold.
   - Ⓕ He has fun on Mars.
   - Ⓖ He is hungry.
   - Ⓗ He doesn't have any friends.

3 **Which event seems real?**
   - Ⓐ There are volcanic craters on
     Mars.
   - Ⓑ Pele goes to school on Mars.
   - Ⓒ Pele's team beat the Martians.
   - Ⓓ Pele lives with a Martian family.

4 **Which sentence has a conjunction?**
   - Ⓔ Mars is like an ice ball.
   - Ⓕ Pele plays crater hockey.
   - Ⓖ The air on Mars is cold.
   - Ⓗ The average temperature is
     −73.4° Fahrenheit, but my
     clothes keep me warm.

5 **What is the story mostly about?**
   - Ⓐ an exchange student's life on
     Mars
   - Ⓑ how to play crater hockey
   - Ⓒ what to wear on Mars
   - Ⓓ where to see Martians

6 **Pele thinks living on Mars is like
   living _____.**
   - Ⓔ with a hockey team
   - Ⓕ in a deep freezer
   - Ⓖ in a crater
   - Ⓗ on Earth

Writing

Directions Look at the following graphic organizer and student writing sample on page 165. Then answer the questions.

Opinion interesting TV show _____

	Description
	made plans to get to moon _____
	equipment needed _____
1	astronauts preparing to go _____

Recommendation 2 _____

---

1 Which picture best fits in box 1?

Ⓐ

2 Fill in blank 2.

Ⓑ

Name _____ Date _____

I watched the show "From Earth to Moon" on Public Television, April 14th.
It was very interesting. (3) _____. It showed all of the equipment
the astronauts needed. (4) _____. I could really feel how nervous
the astronauts were. Anyone who wants to learn about the trips to the moon
should definitely watch this show.

---

3 **Which sentence best fits blank 3?**
  Ⓐ For example, it showed how
     scientists planned to get to the
     moon.
  Ⓑ For example, it showed all the
     cartoons about space flights.
  Ⓒ For example, it had people
     talking about how the moon is
     not made of green cheese.

4 **Which sentence best fits blank 4?**
  Ⓐ Some of the astronauts didn't
     like moon travel.
  Ⓑ The astronauts came back from
     their trip to the moon.
  Ⓒ The astronauts were interviewed
     while preparing for their trip to
     the moon.

5 **Which sentence is the writer's opinion?**
  Ⓐ It was very interesting.
  Ⓑ It showed all of the equipment the astronauts needed.
  Ⓒ I watched the show "From Earth to Moon" on Public Television, April 14th.

The astronauts were excited to get into their spacesuits. The astronauts train, and
they passed tests before they could go.

---

6 **What would make the second sentence in the box above correct?**
  Ⓐ The astronauts train, and they passes tests before they could go.
  Ⓑ The astronauts trained, and they passed tests before they could go.
  Ⓒ The astronauts trains, and passed tests before they could go.

Beginning

Student _____

Teacher _____

Test Section	Skills Tested	Skills/Strategies Tested per item number	Total Scores	Reteaching Tools (For additional reteaching activities, see p. T14)
VOCABULARY *Date Tested:* _____	Words related to space travel and the solar system	1, 2, 3	☐ x 9 points = /27	Newcomer Book Vocabulary Cards Chant Posters TPR Cards Concept Posters Language Practice Academic Language Game Builder Audio CD
GRAMMAR *Date Tested:* _____	Proper Nouns	1, 2, 3, 4	☐ x 8 points = /32	**Proper Nouns:** Teacher's Guide p. 362
READING *Date Tested:* _____	**Comprehension Strategy:** Synthesize **Literary Analysis:** Distinguishes Fantasy from Reality; Similes **Word Study:** Conjunctions	1 2, 4 3	☐ x 8 points = /32	**Comprehension Strategy:** Teacher's Guide p. 373 **Literary Analysis:** Teacher's Guide pp. 369, 379 **Word Study:** Teacher's Guide p. 389
WRITING *Date Tested:* _____	**Writing Form:** Review	1	☐ x 9 points = /9	**Writing Form:** Teacher's Guide pp. 363, 365, 367, 369, 373, 375, 377

SKILLS TO BE DEVELOPED	UNIT 7 Total Score	COMMENTS
  RETEACHING GROUP ASSIGNMENT	/100	
WRITING COMPOSITION EVALUATION *Date Tested:* _____	Obtain individual student writing sample — Teacher's Guide, Week 4 Lesson 4, p. 403 **Figure score using pp. A14–A16** **Composite Score** ☐	See appropriate mini-lessons in the *Writing Resource Guide* and Shared Writing lessons in the Teacher's Guide, pp. 363, 365, 367, 369, 373, 375, 377.

Student Profile | Unit 7 Progress Test

Intermediate/Advanced

Student _____   Teacher _____

Test Section	Skills Tested	Skills/Strategies Tested per item number	Total Scores	Reteaching Tools (For additional reteaching activities, see p. T14)
VOCABULARY *Date Tested:* _____	Words related to space travel and the solar system	1, 2, 3, 4, 5	☐ x 4 points = /20	Newcomer Book Vocabulary Cards Chant Posters TPR Cards Concept Posters Language Practice Game Academic Language Builder Audio CD
GRAMMAR *Date Tested:* _____	Frequency Adverb: *never* Complex Sentences Proper Nouns Comparative	1 2, 5 3 4	☐ x 4 points = /20	**Frequency Adverbs:** Teacher's Guide p. 392 **Complex Sentences:** Teacher's Guide p. 374 **Proper Nouns:** Teacher's Guide p. 362 **Comparative and Superlative:** Teacher's Guide p. 364
READING *Date Tested:* _____	**Comprehension Strategy:** Synthesize **Literary Analysis:** Distinguishes Fantasy from Reality; Similes **Word Study:** Conjunctions	1, 2, 5 3, 6 4	☐ x 5 points = /30	**Comprehension Strategy:** Teacher's Guide p. 373 **Literary Analysis:** Teacher's Guide p. 369, 379 **Word Study:** Teacher's Guide p. 389
WRITING *Date Tested:* _____	**Writing Form:** Review **Written Convention:** Regular and Irregular Past Tense	1, 2, 3, 4, 5 6	☐ x 5 points = /30	**Writing Form:** Teacher's Guide pp. 363, 365, 367, 369, 373, 375, 377 **Written Convention:** Teacher's Guide p. 377

SKILLS TO BE DEVELOPED	UNIT 7 Total Score /100	COMMENTS
RETEACHING GROUP ASSIGNMENT		

| **WRITING COMPOSITION EVALUATION**

Date Tested:
_____ | Obtain individual student writing sample — Teacher's Guide, Week 4 Lesson 4, p. 403 | Figure score using pp. A14–A16

Composite Score ☐ | See appropriate mini-lessons in the *Writing Resource Guide* and Shared Writing lessons in the Teacher's Guide, pp. 363, 365, 367, 369, 373, 375, 377. |

Name _____ Date _____

Things I Know About Reading in English!

When I read a story, I can put information together.

Yes   Sometimes   Not Yet

When I read I can tell what seems real.

Yes   Sometimes   Not Yet

Texts I Can Read in English!

The Moon Olympics

Life is Different in Space!

_____

My Goals:

_____

_____

_____

Things I Can Say in English!

I can talk about the solar system in English.

Yes   Sometimes   Not Yet

I can use proper nouns in English.

Yes   Sometimes   Not Yet

My Goals:

_____

_____

Things I Know About Writing in English!

I can use a chart to plan my review.

Yes   Sometimes   Not Yet

My Goals:

_____

_____

Unit 8
Progress Test

Vocabulary

Pulse of Life

Remind students that this is a test. Tell them that they will complete one test item at a time and that you will read directions for each question.

Sample

Distribute the test page. Point to the sample box. Tell students to look at the pictures in the box as you say and point to each picture: *This picture shows the* moon. *This picture shows* Earth. *This picture shows the* sun. *This picture shows* a crater. Ask *Which picture shows a* crater. Wait for students to respond orally. Say *Bubble* D *is filled in because we were looking for* a crater.

Test Items

Say the following directions for each test item. Then wait for students to bubble in their choice. Tell students to look at you when they are finished with each item.

1. Have students point to item number 1 and say *Look at the pictures in row one. Which picture shows a* voluntary *action?*

   Tell students to bubble in the circle under the picture that shows a *voluntary* action.

2. Have students point to item number 2 and say *Look at the pictures in row two. Which picture shows* respiration?

   Tell students to bubble in the circle under the picture that shows *respiration.*

3. Have students point to item number 3 and say *Look at the pictures in row three. Which picture shows* photosynthesis?

   Tell students to bubble in the circle under the picture that shows *photosynthesis.*

Remind students that this is a test. Tell them that they will complete one test item at a time and that you will read directions for each question.

Sample

Distribute the test page. Point to the sample sentence in the box. Tell students that one word is missing in the sentence. Say *Read this sentence with me. We see* blank *on the moon.* Say *Now we will read the sentence again with each choice to see which one best fits in the blank.*

We see sun *on the moon. We see* craters *on the moon. We see* oxygen *on the moon. We see* Earth *on the moon.* Ask *Which word would make sense to put in the blank?* Wait for students to respond orally. Tell students that bubble *B* is filled in because *We see* craters *on the moon* is the correct choice.

Test Items

Say the following directions for each test item. Then wait for students to bubble in their choice. Tell students to look at you when they are finished with each item.

1. Say *Point to test item 1. Read the sentence with me. Doctors tell patients to drink* blank.

   Then say *Read the sentence and try each word in the blank.*

   Wait for students to read, then say *Bubble in the choice for the word that goes in the blank.*

2. Say *Point to test item 2. Read the sentences with me.* Blank *brings air in and out of the body.*

   Then say *Read the sentence and try each word in the blank.*

   Wait for students to read, then say *Bubble in the choice for the word that goes in the blank.*

3. Say *Point to test item 3. Read the sentence with me. Kicking a ball is a* blank *movement.*

   Then say *Read the sentence and try each word in the blank.*

   Wait for students to read, then say *Bubble in the choice for the word that goes in the blank.*

4. Say *Point to test item 4. Read the sentence with me.* Blank *carry messages between your brain and your other body parts.*

   Then say *Read the sentence and try each word in the blank.*

   Wait for students to read, then say *Bubble in the choice for the word that goes in the blank.*

5. Say *Point to test item 5. Read the sentence with me. A plant uses* blank *to make its own food.*

   Then say *Read the sentence and try each word in the blank.*

   Wait for students to read, then say *Bubble in the choice for the word that goes in the blank.*

Teacher Directions

Grammar

Beginning p. 175

Remind students that this is a test. Tell them that they will complete one test item at a time and that you will read directions for each question.

Sample

Distribute the test page. Point to the sample box. Tell students to look at the pictures in the box as you say and point to each picture: *The label on this picture says* Earth. *The label on this picture says* planets. Ask *Which label shows the proper noun, or the name of the planet?* Wait for students to respond orally. Say *Bubble* A *is filled in because we were looking for the proper noun* Earth.

Test Items

Say the following directions for each test item. Then wait for students to bubble in their choice. Tell students to look at you when they are finished with each item.

1. Have students point to item number 1 and say *Look at the pictures. Listen. Which picture shows* Yippee! It's my birthday today!

   Tell students to bubble in the circle under the picture that shows *Yippee! It's my birthday today!*

2. Have students point to item number 2 and say *Look at the pictures. Listen. Which picture shows* All of these fruits are apples?

   Tell students to bubble in the circle under the picture that shows *All of these fruits are apples.*

3. Have students point to item number 3 and say *Look at the pictures. Listen. Which picture shows* This bottle has only a little bit of water in it?

   Tell students to bubble in the circle under the picture that shows *This bottle has only a little bit of water in it.*

4. Have students point to item number 4 and say *Look at the pictures. Listen. Which picture shows* None of these animals has four legs?

   Tell students to bubble in the circle under the picture that shows *None of these animals has four legs.*

Intermediate p. 179   Advanced p. 183

Remind students that this is a test. Tell them that they will complete one test item at a time and that you will read directions for each question.

Unit 8 Progress Test

Pulse of Life

Sample

Distribute the test page. Point to the sample sentence in the box. Tell students that one word is missing in the sentence. Say *Read this sentence with me.* A cow blank flies. Say *Now we will read the sentence again with each choice to see which one best fits in the blank.* A cow always *flies.* A cow never *flies.* A cow often *flies.* A cow sometimes *flies.* Ask *Which word would make sense to put in the blank?* Wait for students to respond orally. Tell students that bubble *B* is filled in because *A cow never flies* is the correct choice.

Test Items

Say the following directions for each test item. Then wait for students to bubble in their choice. Tell students to look at you when they are finished with each item.

1. Say *Point to test item 1. Read the sentence with me.* Markers, crayons, and paint are blank art supplies. Then say *Read the sentence and try each word in the blank.*

   Wait for students to read, then say *Bubble in the choice for the word that best fits in the blank.*

2. Say *Point to test item 2. Read the sentences with me.* Put the plant in the soil. blank You water it. Then say *Read the answer choices and choose which one shows the correct way to combine the two sentences.*

   Wait for students to read, then say *Bubble in the choice for the correct sentence.*

3. Say *Point to test item 3. Read the sentences with me.* Blank! He runs very fast! Then say *Read the sentences and try each word in the blank.*

   Wait for students to read, then say *Bubble in the choice for the word that best fits in the blank.*

4. Say *Point to test item 4. Read the sentences with me.* Mrs. López will take the food home. blank She pays for it at the store. Then say *Read the answer choices and choose which one shows the correct way to combine the two sentences.*

   Wait for students to read, then say *Bubble in the choice for the correct sentence.*

5. Say *Point to test item 5. Read the sentence with me.* Blank it is winter, there is a lot of snow where Grandma lives. Then say *Read the sentence and try each word in the blank.*

   Wait for students to read, then say *Bubble in the choice for the word that best fits in the blank.*

Beginning pp. 176–177

Remind students that this is a test. Tell them that they will complete one test item at a time and that you will read directions for each question.

Passage

Distribute the reading passage on page 176. Have students point to the pictures in the boxes. Explain that this selection is about the tallest tree in the world. Ask students to follow along as you read the passage aloud. Point to each illustration as you read the corresponding text.

Say *Listen as I read "The Tallest Tree in the World."*

1. Look at picture 1.　　*Wow! This tree is very old! Its branches reach up toward the sky.*

2. Look at picture 2.　　*At first, it was 1 foot, 2 inches tall.*
　　　　　　　　　　　Then it grew to 2 feet, 1 inch.

3. Look at picture 3.　　*Its leaves touch the sun. It drinks rainwater when it is thirsty.*

4. Look at picture 4.　　*As an adult, it is now 274 feet tall. It is the tallest tree in the world.*

Test Items

Distribute test page 177. Say the following directions for each test item. Read aloud the question. Give students time to read and look at the pictures. Then wait for students to bubble in their choice. Tell students to look at you when they are finished with each item.

1. Say *Point to test item 1. Listen to the question. How tall is the tree at the beginning of the story? Look at the pictures and read the answer choices. Bubble in the choice that tells you how tall the tree is at the beginning of the story.*

2. Say *Point to test item 2. Listen to the question. Which sentence tells a strong feeling? Read the answer choices. Bubble in the choice that tells a strong feeling.*

3. Say *Point to test item 3. Listen to the question. Which sentence in the story makes you think of your sense of taste? Look at the pictures and read the answer choices. Bubble in the choice that makes you think of your sense of taste.*

4. Say *Point to test item 4. Listen to the question. Which sentence in the story helps you create a mental image of the tallest tree? Look at the pictures and read the answer choices. Bubble in the choice that helps you create a mental image of the tallest tree.*

Intermediate pp. 180–181
Advanced pp. 184–186

Remind students that this is a test. Explain that they will read the passage on their own and complete the test items.

Passage

Distribute the reading passages. Have students point to the passage. Point to the graphic in the passage. Explain that the graphic information goes with the passage and that they will read this as well as the passage. Tell students that they are going to read about a special tree. Ask students to read the passage independently and to look at you when they are finished.

Test Items

Distribute the test pages. Remind students that they will want to look back at the passage for help in answering questions.

Say *Point to test item 1. Read the question with me. Which sentence makes you think of touching the tree? Read and bubble in the choice that makes you think of your sense of touch.* Wait for students to bubble in their choice. Tell students to look at you when they are finished.

Say *Point to test item 2. Read the question with me. Look at the diagram of the tree. What are the parts of the tree? Read and bubble in the choice that tells the parts of the tree.* Wait for students to bubble in their choice. Tell students to look at you when they are finished.

Tell students to complete the rest of the test themselves.

Teacher Directions | Unit 8 Progress Test

Writing

Pulse of Life

Beginning p. 188

Remind students that this is a test. Tell them that they will complete one test item and that you will read directions for the question. Distribute test page 188. Point to the graphic organizer. Explain that Benita, a fifth-grade student, filled in this chart before writing directions for making a natural snack.

Test Item 1

Point to the first box in the graphic organizer and say *The girl is getting things ready to make a natural food snack.* Point to the second box. Say *She is putting yogurt in the shaker.* Point to the third box. Say *Now she is adding the juice and shaking it.* Point to the last box. Say *Now she is eating the snack.* Point to empty box 1 and say *Look at the pictures. There is one picture missing. It is a picture that shows what she is going to do with the snack when she is done shaking it.* Point to test item 1. Say *Bubble in the choice for the picture that best fits in box 1.* Wait for students to bubble in their choice. Tell students to look at you when they are finished.

Intermediate/Advanced pp. 188–189

Remind students that this is a test. Tell them that they will complete one test item at a time and that you will read directions for each question. Distribute the test pages. Point to the graphic organizer. Explain that Benita, a fifth-grade student, filled in this chart before writing the paragraph about making a natural snack on page 189. Tell them that they will want to use the graphic organizer page and the paragraph that Benita wrote to answer the questions on both pages.

Test Item 1

Point out the missing picture in the graphic organizer. Point to test item 1. Say *Bubble in the choice for the picture that best fits in box 1.* Wait for students to bubble in their choice. Tell students to look at you when they are finished.

Test Item 2

Point to the blank line (2) and then the whole graphic organizer. Say *Label the picture telling what is happening in the last box.* Wait for students to write their answer. Tell students to look at you when they are finished.

Tell students that they are going to read the paragraph that Benita wrote after filling in the chart on page 188. Point to the missing sentences in the writing sample and say *There are two sentences missing.* Tell students to read the paragraph to see what is missing. Wait for students to read the writing sample. Tell students to look at you when they are finished. Remind students to use both the graphic organizer and the paragraph to answer test items 3, 4, and 5.

Test Item 3

Point to test item 3 and say *Read the question and bubble in the choice for blank three.* Wait for students to mark their answers. Tell students to look at you when they are finished.

Test Item 4

Point to test item 4 and say *Read the question and bubble in the choice for blank four.* Wait for students to mark their answers. Tell students to look at you when they are finished.

Test Item 5

Point to test item 5 and say *Read the question and bubble in the best choice.* Wait for students to mark their answers. Tell students to look at you when they are finished.

Test Item 6

Point to the sentences in the box at the bottom section of the page. Say *Benita's friend, Juan, wrote these sentences about the recipe.* Say *Juan's first sentence has a mistake.* Ask students to help Juan fix his sentence. Say *Find the mistake and bubble in the choice for the sentence that would correct it.* Wait for students to mark their answers. Tell students to look at you when they are finished.

Unit 8 Pulse of Life

Vocabulary Ⓑ

Name _____ Date _____

Directions Look at the pictures. Listen to the question. Bubble in the circle underneath the picture for your answer.

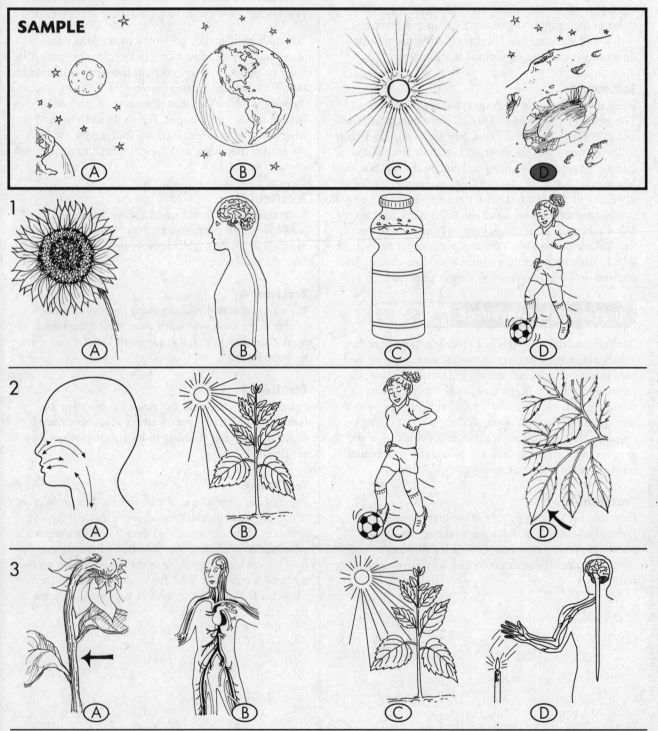

SAMPLE

Ⓐ Ⓑ Ⓒ Ⓓ

1 Ⓐ Ⓑ Ⓒ Ⓓ

2 Ⓐ Ⓑ Ⓒ Ⓓ

3 Ⓐ Ⓑ Ⓒ Ⓓ

Unit 8   Pulse of Life

Grammar Ⓑ

Name _____   Date _____

Directions Look at the pictures. Listen to the question. Bubble in the circle underneath the picture for your answer.

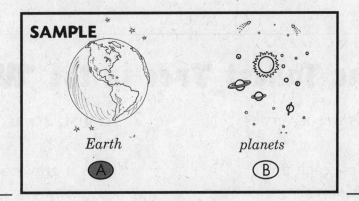

SAMPLE

Earth
Ⓐ

planets
Ⓑ

1

Ⓐ   Ⓑ

3

Ⓐ   Ⓑ

2

Ⓐ   Ⓑ

4
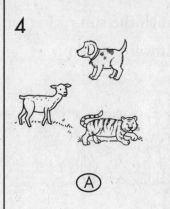
Ⓐ   Ⓑ

Name _____   Date _____

Directions Listen to the selection. Then read each question. Choose the best answer. Bubble in your answer.

The Tallest Tree in the World

1 Wow! This tree is very old!

Its branches reach up toward the sky.

2 At first, it was 1 foot, 2 inches tall.

Then it grew to 2 feet, 1 inch.

Now it is 274 feet tall!

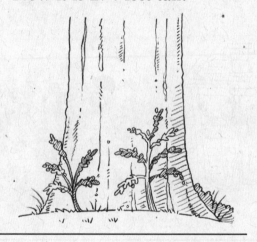

3 Its leaves touch the sun.

It drinks rainwater when it is thirsty.

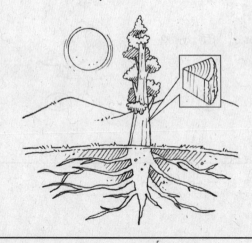

4 As an adult, it is now 274 feet tall.

It is the tallest tree in the world.

Name _____ Date _____

1 How tall is the tree at the beginning of the story?

2 feet, 1 inch	274 feet	1 foot, 2 inches	3 feet, 6 inches
Ⓐ	Ⓑ	Ⓒ	Ⓓ

2 Which sentence tells a strong feeling?

Those are the nutrients.	Its branches reach up toward the sky.	Wow! This tree is very old!	At first, it was 1 foot, 2 inches tall
Ⓐ	Ⓑ	Ⓒ	Ⓓ

3 Which sentence in the story makes you think of your sense of taste?

At first, it was 1 foot, 2 inches tall.	Wow! This tree is very old!	It is now 274 feet tall.	It drinks rainwater when it is thirsty
Ⓐ	Ⓑ	Ⓒ	Ⓓ

4 Which sentence in the story helps you create a mental image of the tallest tree?

At first, it was 1 foot, 2 inches tall.	Wow! This tree is very old!	Its branches reach up toward the sky.	It drinks rainwater when it is thirsty.
Ⓐ	Ⓑ	Ⓒ	Ⓓ

Name _____ Date _____

Directions Read the sentence. Choose the word that best fits in the blank. Bubble in your answer.

SAMPLE

We see _____ on the moon.
- (A) sun
- (B) craters
- (C) oxygen
- (D) space stations

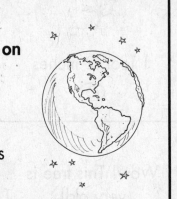

1 Doctors tell patients to drink _____.
- (A) chlorophyll
- (B) fluids
- (C) nutrients
- (D) nerves

2 _____ brings air in and out of the body.
- (E) Photosynthesis
- (F) Respiration
- (G) Emotion
- (H) Chlorophyll

3 Kicking a ball is a _____ movement.
- (A) involuntary
- (B) characteristic
- (C) complex
- (D) voluntary

4 _____ carry messages between your brain and your other body parts.
- (E) Photosynthesis
- (F) Nutrients
- (G) Nerves
- (H) Network

5 A plant uses _____ to make its own food.
- (A) respiration
- (B) nerves
- (C) photosynthesis
- (D) emotion

Name _____ Date _____

Directions Read the sentence. Choose the word that best fits in the blank. For questions 2 and 4, choose the answer that best combines the two sentences. Bubble in your answer.

SAMPLE

A cow _____ flies.

(A) always
(B) never
(C) often
(D) sometimes

1 Markers, crayons, and paint are _____ art supplies.

(A) none
(B) before
(C) all
(D) when

2 **Put the plant in the soil. _____ You water it.**

(E) Put the plant in the soil after you water it.
(F) Put the plant in the soil before you water it.
(G) Put the plant in the soil how you water it.
(H) Put the plant in the soil because you water it.

3 _____! He runs very fast!

(A) Wow
(B) Who
(C) You
(D) Why

4 **Mrs. López will take the food home. _____ She pays for it at the store.**

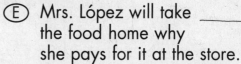

(E) Mrs. López will take the food home why she pays for it at the store.
(F) Mrs. López will take the food home before she pays for it at the store.
(G) Mrs. López will take the food home without she pays for it at the store.
(H) Mrs. López will take the food home after she pays for it at the store.

5 _____ it is winter, there is a lot of snow where Grandma lives.

(A) With
(B) When
(C) And
(D) Who

Name _____ Date _____

The Mighty, Tall Tree!

This tree is the tallest tree in the world. After one year, it was 1 foot, 2 inches tall. It grew to 2 feet, 1 inch tall by age three. As an adult, it is now 274 feet tall. Wow! It can reach heights of 400 feet! Its leaves touch the sun. Sunlight keeps the leaves green. Rainwater keeps the trunk and bark moist. The nutrients are the sun and the rain. It is strong and beautiful.

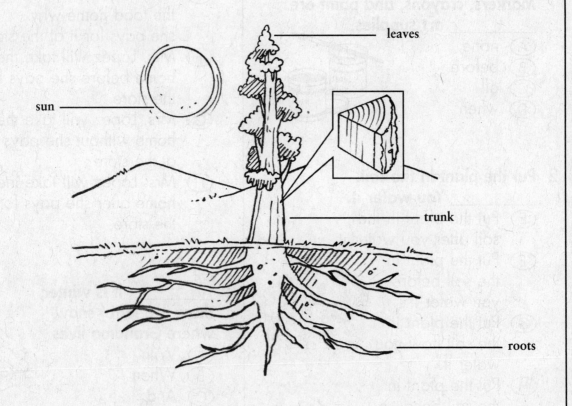

sun

leaves

trunk

roots

Name _____ Date _____

1 **Which sentence makes you think of touching the tree?**
   - (A) This tree is the tallest tree in the world.
   - (B) Wow! It can reach heights of 400 feet!
   - (C) Sunlight keeps the leaves green.
   - (D) Rainwater keeps the trunk and bark moist.

2 **Look at the diagram of the tree. What are the parts of this tree?**
   - (E) petals, flowers, trees
   - (F) trunk, roots, leaves
   - (G) flowers, stem, petals
   - (H) sun, rain, nutrients

3 **Which sentence uses imagery to describe how tall the tree is?**
   - (A) This tree is the tallest tree in the world.
   - (B) The nutrients are the sun and the rain.
   - (C) After one year, it was 1 foot, 2 inches tall.
   - (D) Its leaves touch the sun.

4 **How tall is the tree when it is 3 years old?**
   - (E) 2 feet, 1 inch
   - (F) 274 feet
   - (G) 1 foot, 2 inches
   - (H) 3 feet, 6 inches

5 **Which sentence shows a strong feeling?**
   - (A) After one year, it was 1 foot, 2 inches tall.
   - (B) Wow! It can reach heights of 400 feet!
   - (C) Its leaves touch the sun.
   - (D) The nutrients are the sun and rain.

6 **What sentence in this story helps you create a mental image of the mighty tree?**
   - (E) It grew to 2 feet, 1 inch by age three.
   - (F) After one year, it was 1 foot, 2 inches tall.
   - (G) The nutrients are the sun and the rain.
   - (H) It is strong and beautiful.

Unit 8   Pulse of Life

Vocabulary Ⓐ

Name _____ Date _____

Directions Read the sentences. Choose the word that best fits in the blank. Bubble in your answer.

SAMPLE

We see _____ on the moon.
- Ⓐ sun
- **Ⓑ craters**
- Ⓒ oxygen
- Ⓓ space stations

---

1 Doctors tell patients to drink _____.
- Ⓐ chlorophyll
- Ⓑ fluids
- Ⓒ nutrients
- Ⓓ nerves

2 _____ brings air in and out of the body.
- Ⓔ Photosynthesis
- Ⓕ Respiration
- Ⓖ Emotion
- Ⓗ Chlorophyll

3 Kicking a ball is a _____ movement.
- Ⓐ involuntary
- Ⓑ characteristic
- Ⓒ complex
- Ⓓ voluntary

4 _____ carry messages between your brain and your other body parts.
- Ⓔ Photosynthesis
- Ⓕ Nutrients
- Ⓖ Nerves
- Ⓗ Network

5 A plant uses _____ to make its own food.
- Ⓐ respiration
- Ⓑ nerves
- Ⓒ photosynthesis
- Ⓓ emotion

Unit 8 Pulse of Life

Name _____ Date _____

Directions Read the sentence. Choose the word that best fits in the blank. For questions 2 and 4, choose the answer that best combines the two sentences. Bubble in your answer.

SAMPLE

A cow _____ flies.
- Ⓐ always
- **Ⓑ never**
- Ⓒ often
- Ⓓ sometimes

---

1 **Markers, crayons, and paint are _____ art supplies.**
- Ⓐ none
- Ⓑ before
- Ⓒ all
- Ⓓ when

2 **Put the plant in the soil. _____ You water it.**
- Ⓔ Put the plant in the soil after you water it.
- Ⓕ Put the plant in the soil before you water it.
- Ⓖ Put the plant in the soil how you water it.
- Ⓗ Put the plant in the soil because you water it.

3 **_____! He runs very fast!**
- Ⓐ Wow
- Ⓑ Who
- Ⓒ You
- Ⓓ Why

4 **Mrs. López will take the food home. _____ She pays for it at the store.**
- Ⓔ Mrs. López will take the food home why she pays for it at the store.
- Ⓕ Mrs. López will take the food home before she pays for it at the store.
- Ⓖ Mrs. López will take the food home without she pays for it at the store.
- Ⓗ Mrs. López will take the food home after she pays for it at the store.

5 **_____ it is winter, there is a lot of snow where Grandma lives.**
- Ⓐ With
- Ⓑ When
- Ⓒ And
- Ⓓ Who

Name _____ Date _____

Directions Read the selection. Then read each question. Choose the best answer. Bubble in your answer.

Mother Nature's Mighty Tree!

This tree is the tallest tree in the world. When it was a year old, it was 1 foot, 2 inches tall. By age three, it had grown to 2 feet, 1 inch tall. It now has reached the height of 274 feet. This tree is not finished growing. Wow! It can reach heights of 400 feet! Its leaves touch the sun.

Sunlight keeps the leaves green. Without sunlight, the leaves wilt and turn dry. Rainwater keeps the trunk and bark moist. The tree drinks rainwater when it is thirsty. We look at that tree and admire its beauty. It is strong and beautiful. It is a wonderful example of Mother Nature at its best.

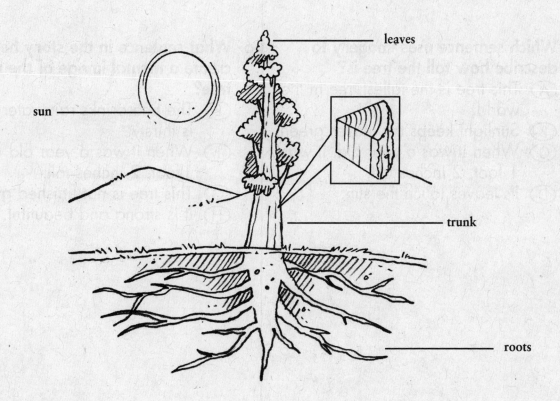

leaves

sun

trunk

roots

Unit 8 Pulse of Life   Reading Ⓐ

Name _____ Date _____

1 **Which sentence makes you think of touching the tree?**
   Ⓐ This tree is the tallest tree in the world.
   Ⓑ Wow! It can reach heights of 400 feet!
   Ⓒ Sunlight keeps the leaves green.
   Ⓓ Rainwater keeps the trunk and bark moist.

2 **Look at the diagram of the tree. What are the parts of this tree?**
   Ⓔ petals, flowers, trees
   Ⓕ trunk, roots, leaves
   Ⓖ flowers, stem, petals
   Ⓗ sun, rain, nutrients

3 **Which sentence uses imagery to describe how tall the tree is?**
   Ⓐ This tree is the tallest tree in the world.
   Ⓑ Sunlight keeps the leaves green.
   Ⓒ When it was a year old, it was 1 foot, 2 inches tall.
   Ⓓ Its leaves touch the sun.

4 **How tall is the tree when it is 3 years old?**
   Ⓔ 2 feet, 1 inch
   Ⓕ 274 feet
   Ⓖ 1 foot, 2 inches
   Ⓗ 3 feet, 6 inches

5 **Which sentence shows a strong feeling?**
   Ⓐ When it was a year old, it was 1 foot, 2 inches tall.
   Ⓑ Wow! It can reach heights of 400 feet!
   Ⓒ Its leaves touch the sun.
   Ⓓ The tree drinks rainwater when it is thirsty.

6 **What sentence in the story helps you create a mental image of the mighty tree?**
   Ⓔ The tree drinks rainwater when it is thirsty.
   Ⓕ When it was a year old, it was 1 foot, 2 inches tall.
   Ⓖ This tree is not finished growing.
   Ⓗ It is strong and beautiful.

Writing

Name _____ Date _____

Directions Look at the following graphic organizer and student sample writing on page 189. Then answer the questions.

Get the ingredients. _____

Put yogurt in shaker. _____

Add juice and shake. _____

1 _____ Pour and freeze. _____

2 _____

---

1 **Which picture best fits in box 1?**

2 **Fill in blank 2.**

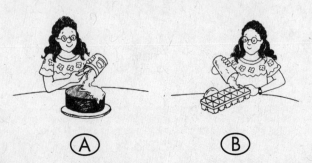

Ⓐ   Ⓑ

Name _____ Date _____

I want to make a delicious healthy frozen snack. You can make it too. Just follow these steps. (3) _____. Next put in a half of a cup of yogurt. (4) _____. Finally, pour the liquid into ice cube trays and freeze. When you're hungry, take the juice cubes out and eat a healthy frozen snack!

---

3 Which sentence best fits in blank 3?
- Ⓐ Then get a towel, clean off the counter, and get something to drink.
- Ⓑ First get out a shaker, yogurt, and fruit juice.
- Ⓒ Next add a tablespoon of sugar and mix well.

4 Which sentence best fits in blank 4?
- Ⓐ After that, add a cup of juice and shake the ingredients.
- Ⓑ After that, eat two cups of chocolate ice cream.
- Ⓒ After that, bake it for one hour.

5 What is the last step for making a frozen snack?
- Ⓐ make a delicious healthy snack
- Ⓑ add half of a cup of yogort
- Ⓒ pour liquid into ice trays and freeze

Before I pour the liquid into the trays, I freeze it. Then I wait.

---

6 What would make the first sentence in the box above correct?
- Ⓐ When I pour the liquid into the trays, I freeze it.
- Ⓑ After I pour the liquid into the trays, I freeze it.
- Ⓒ Now I pour the liquid into the trays, I freeze it.

Student Profile | Unit 8 Progress Test

Beginning

Student _____

Teacher _____

Test Section	Skills Tested	Skills/Strategies Tested per item number	Total Scores	Reteaching Tools (For additional reteaching activities, see p. T14)	
VOCABULARY *Date Tested:* _____	Words related to plants and the human body	1, 2, 3	☐ x 9 points = **/27**	Newcomer Book Chant Posters Concept Posters Academic Language Builder	TPR Cards Vocabulary Cards Language Practice Game Audio CD

GRAMMAR
Date Tested:
_____
	Interjections
	
	Quantity Words:
	all, a little, none
		1
		
		2, 3, 4
			☐
			x
			8 points
			=
			/32
				Interjections:
				  Teacher's Guide p. 422
				Quantity Words:
				  Teacher's Guide p. 432	

READING
Date Tested:
_____
	Literary Analysis:
	  Descriptive Language and Imagery
	Word Study: Interjections
	Comprehension Strategy: Create Images
		1
		
		2
		3, 4
			☐
			x
			8 points
			=
			/32
				Literarcy Analysis:
				  Teacher's Guide p. 427
				Word Study:
				  Teacher's Guide p. 437
				Comprehension Strategy:
				  Teacher's Guide p. 430	

WRITING
Date Tested:
_____
	Writing Form:
	  Procedural
		1	☐
			x
			9 points
			=
			/9
				Writing Form:
				  Teacher's Guide pp. 421, 423, 425, 427, 431, 433, 435	

SKILLS TO BE DEVELOPED	UNIT 8 Total Score **/100**	COMMENTS
RETEACHING GROUP ASSIGNMENT		

| **WRITING COMPOSITION EVALUATION**
Date Tested:
_____ | Obtain individual student writing sample — Teacher's Guide, Week 4 Lesson 4, p. 461 | Figure score using pp. A14–A16

Composite Score ☐ | See appropriate mini-lessons in the *Writing Resource Guide* and Shared Writing lessons in the Teacher's Guide, pp. 421, 423, 425, 427, 431, 433, 435. |

Intermediate/Advanced

Student _____

Teacher _____

Item Analysis

Test Section	Skills Tested	Skills/Strategies Tested per item number	Total Scores	Reteaching Tools (For additional reteaching activities, see p. T14)
VOCABULARY Date Tested: _____	Words related to plants and the human body	1, 2, 3, 4, 5	☐ x 4 points = ☐ /20	Newcomer Book TPR Cards Chant Posters Vocabulary Cards Concept Posters Language Practice Game Academic Language Builder Audio CD
GRAMMAR Date Tested: _____	Quantity Word: *all* Sentence Combining with *before* and *after* Interjections Clauses with *when*	1 2, 4 3 5	☐ x 4 points = ☐ /20	**Quantity Words:** Teacher's Guide p. 432 **Sentence Combining with *after, before* and *when*:** Teacher's Guide p. 450 **Interjections:** Teacher's Guide p. 422 **Clauses with *after, before* and *when*:** Teacher's Guide p. 420
READING Date Tested: _____	**Comprehension Strategy:** Create Images **Nonfiction Text Feature:** Labels **Literary Analysis:** Descriptive Language and imagery **Word Study:** Interjections	1, 6 2 3, 4 5	☐ x 5 points = ☐ /30	**Comprehension Strategy:** Teacher's Guide p. 430 **Nonfiction Text Feature:** Teacher's Guide p. 437 **Literacy Analysis:** Teacher's Guide p. 427 **Word Study:** Teacher's Guide p. 437
WRITING Date Tested: _____	**Writing Form:** Procedural **Written Convention:** Clauses with *after, before,* and *when*	1, 2, 3, 4, 5 6	☐ x 5 points = ☐ /30	**Writing Form:** Teacher's Guide pp. 421, 423, 425, 427, 431, 433, 435 **Written Convention:** Teacher's Guide p. 435
SKILLS TO BE DEVELOPED **RETEACHING GROUP ASSIGNMENT**		**UNIT 8 Total Score** ☐ /100		**COMMENTS**
WRITING COMPOSITION EVALUATION Date Tested: _____	Obtain individual student writing sample — Teacher's Guide, Week 4 Lesson 4, p. 461	Figure score using pp. A14–A16 **Composite Score** ☐		See appropriate mini-lessons in the *Writing Resource Guide* and Shared Writing lessons in the Teacher's Guide, pp. 421, 423, 425, 427, 431, 433, 435.

Name _____ Date _____

Things I Know About Reading in English!

When I read a story, I can form pictures in my mind.

Yes   **Sometimes**   **Not Yet**

When I read I can think about descriptions.

Yes   **Sometimes**   **Not Yet**

Texts I Can Read in English!

Plants Are Alive!

The Rap About the Nervous

System

My Goals:

_____

_____

_____

Things I Can Say in English!

I can talk about the human body in English.

Yes   **Sometimes**   **Not Yet**

I can use words to say "how many" in English.

Yes   **Sometimes**   **Not Yet**

My Goals:

_____

_____

_____

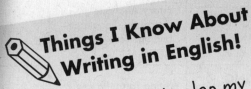

Things I Know About Writing in English!

I can use a chart to plan my set of instructions.

Yes   **Sometimes**   **Not Yet**

My Goals:

_____

_____

_____

Answer Key | Unit 1

Vocabulary

B p. 6

1 D
2 B
3 B

I p. 10

1 C
2 F
3 C
4 H
5 D

A p. 14

1 C
2 F
3 C
4 H
5 D

Grammar

B p. 7

1 A
2 B
3 A
4 B

I p. 11

1 C
2 E
3 C
4 E
5 B

A p. 15

1 C
2 E
3 C
4 E
5 B

Reading Comprehension

B pp. 8–9

1 E
2 D
3 D
4 C

I pp. 12–13

1 B
2 E
3 C
4 F
5 C
6 F

A pp. 16–18

1 B
2 E
3 C
4 F
5 C
6 H

Writing

B p. 20

1 B

I **A** pp. 20–21

1 B
2 Possible Answer: Your
3 B
4 A
5 C
6 B

Answer Key Unit 2

Vocabulary

B p. 30
1 D
2 A
3 C

I p. 34
1 B
2 E
3 C
4 E
5 D

A p. 38
1 B
2 E
3 C
4 E
5 D

Grammar

B p. 31
1 A
2 A
3 A
4 B

I p. 35
1 B
2 G
3 D
4 E
5 B

A p. 39
1 B
2 G
3 D
4 E
5 B

Reading Comprehension

B pp. 32–33
1 A
2 D
3 B
4 A

I pp. 36–37
1 B
2 E
3 C
4 H
5 D
6 G

A pp. 40–42
1 B
2 E
3 C
4 H
5 D
6 G

Writing

B p. 44
1 B

I A pp. 44–45
1 B
2 Possible Answers: Sincerely,; Truly yours,;
  A concerned citizen,
3 B
4 A
5 A
6 A

Answer Key | Unit 3

Vocabulary

B p. 54

1 C
2 C
3 C

I p. 58

1 D
2 E
3 D
4 G
5 C

A p. 62

1 D
2 E
3 D
4 G
5 C

Grammar

B p. 55

1 A
2 A
3 B
4 B

I p. 59

1 D
2 F
3 A
4 G
5 B

A p. 63

1 D
2 F
3 A
4 G
5 B

Reading Comprehension

B pp. 56–57

1 D
2 B
3 B
4 B

I pp. 60–61

1 B
2 H
3 B
4 G
5 C
6 E

A pp. 64–66

1 B
2 H
3 B
4 G
5 C
6 E

Writing

B p. 68

1 A

I A pp. 68–69

1 A
2 Possible Answers: heard drums go boom-boom; players made drums go boom-boom
3 A
4 C
5 C
6 B

Answer Key | Unit 4

Vocabulary

B p. 78

1 D
2 B
3 A

I p. 82

1 C
2 E
3 D
4 F
5 A

A p. 86

1 C
2 E
3 D
4 F
5 A

Grammar

B p. 79

1 B
2 A
3 B
4 A

I p. 83

1 B
2 G
3 A
4 F
5 D

A p. 87

1 B
2 G
3 A
4 F
5 A

Reading Comprehension

B pp. 80–81

1 B
2 A
3 C
4 B

I pp. 84–85

1 A
2 F
3 C
4 G
5 D
6 H

A pp. 88–90

1 A
2 F
3 C
4 G
5 D
6 H

Writing

B p. 92

1 A

I A pp. 92–93

1 A
2 Possible Answer: Kuhli Loach
3 C
4 A
5 B
6 C

Answer Key | Unit 5

Vocabulary

B p. 102
1 A
2 C
3 B

I p. 106
1 C
2 F
3 A
4 G
5 C

A p. 110
1 C
2 F
3 A
4 G
5 C

Grammar

B p. 103
1 A
2 B
3 B
4 A

I p. 107
1 C
2 G
3 C
4 H
5 D

A p. 111
1 C
2 G
3 C
4 H
5 D

Reading Comprehension

B pp. 104–105
1 B
2 A
3 C
4 B

I pp. 108–109
1 B
2 F
3 B
4 H
5 A
6 E

A pp. 112–114
1 B
2 F
3 B
4 H
5 A
6 E

Writing

B p. 116
1 A

I A pp. 116–117
1 A
2 Possible Answer: Life was lonely and difficult.
3 B
4 C
5 B
6 C

Answer Key   Unit 6

Vocabulary

B p. 126
1 B
2 C
3 A

I p. 130
1 A
2 F
3 D
4 G
5 C

A p. 134
1 A
2 F
3 D
4 G
5 C

Grammar

B p. 127
1 B
2 A
3 A
4 B

I p. 131
1 C
2 E
3 D
4 G
5 A

A p. 135
1 C
2 E
3 D
4 G
5 A

Reading Comprehension

B pp. 128–129
1 D
2 A
3 D
4 B

I pp. 132–133
1 D
2 H
3 A
4 F
5 A
6 E

A pp. 136–138
1 D
2 H
3 A
4 F
5 A
6 E

Writing

B p. 140
1 B

I **A** pp. 140–141
1 B
2 Possible Answer: supporting details
3 C
4 B
5 A
6 C

Answer Key Unit 7

Vocabulary

B p. 150
1 D
2 D
3 D

I p. 154
1 A
2 F
3 A
4 E
5 B

A p. 158
1 A
2 F
3 A
4 E
5 B

Grammar

B p. 151
1 A
2 A
3 B
4 A

I p. 155
1 B
2 E
3 C
4 E
5 D

A p. 159
1 B
2 E
3 C
4 E
5 D

Reading Comprehension

B pp. 152–153
1 B
2 D
3 D
4 A

I pp. 156–157
1 B
2 F
3 A
4 H
5 A
6 F

A pp. 160–162
1 B
2 F
3 A
4 H
5 A
6 F

Writing

B p. 164
1 A

I **A** pp. 164–165
1 A
2 Possible Answer: watch this show
3 A
4 C
5 C
6 B

Answer Key Unit 8

Vocabulary

B p. 174

1 D
2 A
3 C

I p. 178

1 B
2 F
3 D
4 G
5 C

A p. 182

1 B
2 F
3 D
4 G
5 C

Grammar

B p. 175

1 B
2 A
3 A
4 B

I p. 179

1 C
2 F
3 A
4 H
5 B

A p. 183

1 C
2 F
3 A
4 H
5 B

Reading Comprehension

B pp. 176–177

1 C
2 C
3 D
4 C

I pp. 180–181

1 D
2 F
3 D
4 E
5 B
6 H

A pp. 184–186

1 D
2 F
3 D
4 E
5 B
6 H

Writing

B p. 188

1 B

I A pp. 188–189

1 B
2 Possible Answer: Take out juice cubes; eat.
3 B
4 A
5 C
6 B

Stages of Language Acquisition

Beginning	Intermediate	
Stage 1: **Preproduction**	**Stage 2:** **Early Production**	**Stage 3:** **Speech Emergence**
Comprehension Understands little of everyday English. **Message** Communicates primarily through gestures or single-word utterances. Able to communicate only the most rudimentary needs. **Fluency and Sentence Structure** Produces little, if any, spoken English.	**Comprehension** Understands some social conversation but limited academic conversation. **Message** Uses routine expressions to convey basic needs and ideas. To some extent, continues to rely on gestures to communicate. **Fluency and Sentence Structure** Uses some basic words and simple phrases. **Word Choice and Academic Language** Relies on routine language expressions. May use some academic words in isolation.	**Comprehension** Understands most of what is said in social and academic conversation but exhibits occasional lack of understanding. **Message** Participates in everyday conversations about familiar topics. Although speech contains errors that sometimes hinder communication, student can often convey his or her basic message. **Fluency and Sentence Structure** Produces longer, complete phrases and some sentences. **Word Choice and Academic Language** Relies on high-frequency words and sometimes cannot fully communicate ideas due to a lack of sufficient vocabulary. Uses some academic language although not always successfully.

Advanced

Stage 4: Intermediate Fluency	Stage 5: Advanced Fluency
Comprehension Rarely experiences a lack of understanding in social and academic situations. **Message** Engages in ordinary conversation. Although errors may be present, they generally do not hinder communication. Successfully communicates most ideas to others. **Fluency and Sentence Structure** Engages in ordinary conversation with some complex sentences. Errors no longer hinder communication. **Word Choice and Academic Language** Range of vocabulary and academic language allows student to communicate well on everyday topics. Begins to use idioms. Occasionally uses inappropriate terms and/or must rephrase to work around unknown vocabulary.	**Comprehension** Understands social and academic conversation without difficulty. **Message** Uses English successfully to convey his or her ideas to others. **Fluency and Sentence Structure** Speech appears to be fluent and effortless, approximating that of native-speaking peers. **Word Choice and Academic Language** Use of vocabulary, academic language, and idioms approximate that of native-speaking peers.

Assessing Reading Fluency

"Reading fluency is... a critical component to ensure successful reading comprehension." (National Reading Panel, 2000)

Fluent readers read texts accurately and quickly with expression. They read expressively by dividing the text into meaningful phrases and clauses, knowing when to pause appropriately within and at the end of sentences, and changing emphasis and tone while reading. Reading fluently facilitates reading connected text and thereby supports comprehension, as students recognize words quickly and accurately while reading with expression.

The *On Our Way to English* Assessment Handbook provides the tools necessary for assessing reading fluency with English language learners in order to track development over time (See pp. 47–48 of the *On Our Way to English* Assessment Handbook).

Assessment Tool	Grades	Materials	Throughout the Year	End of the Year
Reading Fluency Assessment	K–5 (Stages 4 & 5)	*On Our Way to English* Assessment Handbook: pp. 47–48 .... *On Our Way to English* Leveled Reading Teacher's Guide: Leveled Reading Books	Every 4–6 weeks with a Leveled Reading Book	Last month of school

The Leveled or Guided Reading books in *On Our Way to English* are read two times in each lesson, providing students an opportunity to practice fluent reading skills as the teacher coaches. To assess reading fluency, the student practices reading the books an additional two to three times before reading aloud to the teacher, who assesses with a fluency rubric and times the reading.

Reading fluency is assessed only with students in Stages 4–5 because oral reading ability relies heavily on fluent oral speaking ability. For English language learners in Stages 1–3, *On Our Way to English* emphasizes research-proven techniques and materials that accelerate oral language fluency, building the foundation for reading fluency.

Developing Reading Fluency

Leveled or Guided Reading provides systematic modeling, feedback, and support, which are key research-based instructional techniques for success with developing reading fluency. Multiple readings provide fluency practice.

Student Anthologies support reading fluency development because students are reading along with a more fluent reader, the teacher—a research proven technique. Subsequent rereading opportunities provide additional fluency practice as students revisit reading Student Anthologies during centers or independent reading.

Newcomer Books feature echo reading and choral reading, techniques that allow Beginners to hear fluent English and to practice imitating fluent phrasing and pronunciation—key reading fluency practices.

Chant Posters (with Audio CDs) make use of chants, rhymes, and rhythm to support reading fluency. Students can use these for repeated reading practice, listening, or chanting along. The patterned language in these materials facilitates the development of phrasing, intonation, and expression—all valuable skills for the development of reading fluency, while building vocabulary and English oral language.

Writing Rubric

Use the following writing rubric in evaluating the writing of your English language learners. The rubric was designed specifically with English language learners in mind and focuses on providing criteria for evaluating informational writing, the focus of the *On Our Way to English* program.

Emergent		Early	
Writing Level 1	**Writing Level 2**	**Writing Level 3**	
Message and Content Unable to respond or draws a picture or dictates a message (in English or primary language). **Conventions of English** May know the direction that print goes and use some conventional symbols in a random fashion.	**Message and Content** Copies environmental print or labels drawings or writes a simple message. **Conventions of English** Begins to use spacing between words and sound-symbol relationships to produce temporary spelling. **Word Choice and Academic Language** May use isolated academic terms in labeling or dictation.	**Message and Content** With the support of a graphic organizer and a topic about which he or she can produce connected oral discourse, the student produces phrases or sentences that convey a message on one topic. **Conventions of English** Uses sound-symbol relationships to spell and groups words in phrases or sentences. Begins to use uppercase and lowercase conventionally. May make spelling errors that reflect his or her nonnative English pronunciation or native-language spelling patterns. **Word Choice and Academic Language** If academic language is included, it is often used inappropriately or imprecisely. **Fluency and Sentence Structure** Phrases or sentences can generally be understood by adults but may be repetitive and simple. Word order may reflect native-language word order.	

There are four areas of evaluation within the levels: Message and Content, Conventions of English, Word Choice and Academic Language, and Fluency and Sentence Structure. The first two writing levels use only some of these areas since all are not appropriate.

Early Fluency		Fluency
Writing Level 4	**Writing Level 5**	**Writing Level 6**

Message and Content With the support of a graphic organizer, the student produces a piece of writing that has a beginning, middle, and end, as well as sentences on a single topic.	**Message and Content** With the support of a graphic organizer, the student writes several paragraphs with cohesive structure and connected sentences.	**Message and Content** Writes several pages with paragraphs in logical sequence and descriptions that are coherently developed.
Conventions of English Spells words in common word families and uses most punctuation conventionally.	**Conventions of Spelling** Uses spelling and punctuation accurately. Uses verb tenses and first/third person appropriately. May experiment with more complex verb forms.	**Conventions of English** Has control of conventions appropriate to grade level. Uses complex verb forms skillfully.
Word Choice and Academic Language Shows a range of vocabulary and varied word choice with some academic language used appropriately.	**Word Choice and Academic Language** Selects vocabulary, including academic language, appropriately and according to audience and purpose.	**Word Choice and Academic Language** Uses a wide range of vocabulary appropriate to audience, purpose, and style. Uses grade-level academic language effectively.
Fluency and Sentence Structure Word order generally reflects English word order. Sentences may be simple but complete and perhaps loosely connected to one another or run-ons.	**Fluency and Sentence Structure** Uses some compound sentences with conjunctions. Begins to use connecting words, although perhaps, inconsistently or inappropriately.	**Fluency and Sentence Structure** Uses a range of sentence structures, including complex sentences. Uses connecting words effectively.

Writing Assessment Summary Sheet

Student _____ Grade _____ School Year _____

At the end of each Thematic Unit, assess students' writing samples using the Writing Rubric on pages A14 and A15 of this book. Make a photocopy of this page for each student, noting the student's name, grade, and academic year on the sheet. Above each Unit's column note the student's Writing Level determined with the Writing Rubric. Then in each row of that column, fill in the next Writing Level and evaluate students' progress toward that new expectation within each category. When students meet the expectations in all four categories, they have moved on to the next Writing Level.

Skill	Unit 1	Unit 2	Unit 3	Unit 4	Unit 5	Unit 6	Unit 7	Unit 8
Message and Content (Writing Levels 1–6)	Does student meet the expectations for Writing Level ___? ☐ Yes ☐ No	Does student meet the expectations for Writing Level ___? ☐ Yes ☐ No	Does student meet the expectations for Writing Level ___? ☐ Yes ☐ No	Does student meet the expectations for Writing Level ___? ☐ Yes ☐ No	Does student meet the expectations for Writing Level ___? ☐ Yes ☐ No	Does student meet the expectations for Writing Level ___? ☐ Yes ☐ No	Does student meet the expectations for Writing Level ___? ☐ Yes ☐ No	Does student meet the expectations for Writing Level ___? ☐ Yes ☐ No
Conventions of English (Writing Levels 1–6)	Does student meet the expectations for Writing Level ___? ☐ Yes ☐ No	Does student meet the expectations for Writing Level ___? ☐ Yes ☐ No	Does student meet the expectations for Writing Level ___? ☐ Yes ☐ No	Does student meet the expectations for Writing Level ___? ☐ Yes ☐ No	Does student meet the expectations for Writing Level ___? ☐ Yes ☐ No	Does student meet the expectations for Writing Level ___? ☐ Yes ☐ No	Does student meet the expectations for Writing Level ___? ☐ Yes ☐ No	Does student meet the expectations for Writing Level ___? ☐ Yes ☐ No
Word Choice and Academic Language (Writing Levels 2–6)	Does student meet the expectations for Writing Level ___? ☐ Yes ☐ No	Does student meet the expectations for Writing Level ___? ☐ Yes ☐ No	Does student meet the expectations for Writing Level ___? ☐ Yes ☐ No	Does student meet the expectations for Writing Level ___? ☐ Yes ☐ No	Does student meet the expectations for Writing Level ___? ☐ Yes ☐ No	Does student meet the expectations for Writing Level ___? ☐ Yes ☐ No	Does student meet the expectations for Writing Level ___? ☐ Yes ☐ No	Does student meet the expectations for Writing Level ___? ☐ Yes ☐ No
Fluency and Sentence Structure (Writing Levels 3–6)	Does student meet the expectations for Writing Level ___? ☐ Yes ☐ No	Does student meet the expectations for Writing Level ___? ☐ Yes ☐ No	Does student meet the expectations for Writing Level ___? ☐ Yes ☐ No	Does student meet the expectations for Writing Level ___? ☐ Yes ☐ No	Does student meet the expectations for Writing Level ___? ☐ Yes ☐ No	Does student meet the expectations for Writing Level ___? ☐ Yes ☐ No	Does student meet the expectations for Writing Level ___? ☐ Yes ☐ No	Does student meet the expectations for Writing Level ___? ☐ Yes ☐ No

Student Summary Profiles

Student _____ Teacher _____ School Year _____

DIRECTIONS Use each Unit Progress Test Student Profile to record the level of unit test administered and the unit test total score in the two columns under each unit below. Also record below the Writing Composition Composite score from each Unit Test Student Profile.

Section Tested	UNIT 1 Level ☐ Score	UNIT 2 Level ☐ Score	UNIT 3 Level ☐ Score	UNIT 4 Level ☐ Score	UNIT 5 Level ☐ Score	UNIT 6 Level ☐ Score	UNIT 7 Level ☐ Score	UNIT 8 Level ☐ Score
VOCABULARY								
GRAMMAR								
READING								
WRITING FORM/ CONVENTIONS								
UNIT TEST TOTAL	/100	/100	/100	/100	/100	/100	/100	/100
WRITING COMPOSTION COMPOSITE SCORE								
COMMENTS								

ADEQUATE YEARLY PROGRESS

READING LEVEL
Record below results from assessments administered at the beginning, middle, and end of the year, using the *Rigby ELL Assessment Kit.*

Reading Proficiency Report

Beginning of Year	Middle of Year	End of Year
Level _____	Level _____	Level _____

WRITING LEVEL
Record below the Writing Composition Composite Score from Unit 1 (beginning of year) and Unit 8 (end of year).

Writing Composition Composite Score

Beginning of Year	End of Year

ORAL LANGUAGE STAGE
Assess Stage of Oral Language Development using Pre- and Post-Retelling Assessments (see Assessment Handbook). Record below the date of assessment and circle the Stage of Oral Language Development corresponding to the date of assessment.

Pre-Retelling Date:	1	2	3	4	5
Post-Retelling Date:	1	2	3	4	5

Open-Ended Oral Language Assessment

Reassess students' Language Acquisition Stages. Begin with an open-ended prompt like the first one below. If students are unable to respond, intervene with increasingly directed prompts, such as the second and third ones below.

What can you tell me about this picture?

What are the people doing?

I see people protesting. What do you see people doing?

Assessment Directions: Copy this form for each student and place the completed form in the student's portfolio. Locate the student's Language Acquisition Stage for each of the first four activities and assess his or her performance during the unit according to expectations for that Stage. For the Class Collection retelling, pull students to retell the main selection during end-of-unit assessment time. Use the Open-Ended Oral Language Assessment to reassess students' Language Acquisition Stages with one-fourth of your students for each unit, using the back side of the sheet to take notes. For more guidance on assessment, see the Assessment Handbook or the ELL Assessment Kit.

Unit 1 Assessment

Name _____   Date _____

On Our Way to English Grade 5

STAGE EXPECTATIONS

	❶	❷	❸	❹	❺
Content Area Knowledge Language Practice Game, Skills Masters, Page 14 How does the student demonstrate a knowledge of verbs related to freedoms?	Matches cards and sometimes says the word. ☐ Yes ☐ Not yet	Matches cards and usually says the word. ☐ Yes ☐ Not yet	Matches cards and completes key sentence pattern, *I am free to ___*. ☐ Yes ☐ Not yet	Matches card and extends the key sentence using a so/because clause, such as *I am free to learn, so I go to school*. ☐ Yes ☐ Not yet	
Social Language Function Ask for Assistance or Permission, Thematic Teacher's Guide, page 44 How does the student respond during the lesson?	Uses gestures, such as pointing, and possibly the phrase *May I?* to ask for assistance or permission related to classroom activities. ☐ Yes ☐ Not yet		Uses simple sentences to ask for assistance or permission, such as *May I use?* or *Please show me*. ☐ Yes ☐ Not yet	Uses complete, complex sentences to ask for assistance or permission in the classroom, such as *Please show me how to fold this paper or May I go to the library and check out a book?* ☐ Yes ☐ Not yet	
Academic Discussion Strategy Listen and Restate Someone's Comments, Thematic Teacher's Guide, page 32 How does the student respond during the lesson?			Restates someone's comments from the reading, using simple sentences, such as *Dolley says sorry*. ☐ Yes ☐ Not yet	Restates someone's comments from the main selection, using complete sentences, such as *Dolley says that she is worried. She thinks that her father will have to go to war*. ☐ Yes ☐ Not yet	
Anthology Retelling Thematic Teacher's Guide, pp. 50–55 Have each student use the back flap to retell the main selection. How does the student retell the selection?	Uses the Character Web to point to the pictures of Dolley in the correct order. ☐ Yes ☐ Not yet	Points to the pictures in the order the character experienced the feelings and uses a few words. ☐ Yes ☐ Not yet	Retells using longer phrases or simple sentences. ☐ Yes ☐ Not yet	Retells using complete sentences in connected discourse with few errors. ☐ Yes ☐ Not yet	Retells using language similar to native English-speaking peers. ☐ Yes ☐ Not yet
Open-Ended Oral Language Assessment, page A19 Use the student's responses to the illustration to reassess the student's Stage of Language Acquisition.	☐ **STAGE ❶** Uses few or no words; gestures or points.	☐ **STAGE ❷** Uses words or short phrases.	☐ **STAGE ❸** Uses phrases and simple sentences.	☐ **STAGE ❹** Uses sentences in connected discourse.	☐ **STAGE ❺** Uses language comparable to native-speaking peers.

Open-Ended Oral Language Assessment

Reassess students' Language Acquisition Stages. Begin with an open-ended prompt like the first one below. If students are unable to respond, intervene with increasingly directed prompts, such as the second and third ones below.

What can you tell me about this picture?

What people and buildings do you see?

I see senators at the capitol. Who do you see?

Assessment Directions: Copy this form for each student and place the completed form in the student's portfolio. Locate the student's Language Acquisition Stage for each of the first four activities and assess his or her performance during the unit according to expectations for that Stage. For the Class Collection retelling, pull students to retell the main selection during end-of-unit assessment time. Use the Open-Ended Oral Language Assessment to reassess students' Language Acquisition Stages with one-fourth of your students for each unit, using the back side of the sheet to take notes. For more guidance on assessment, see the Assessment Handbook or the ELL Assessment Kit.

Unit 2 Assessment

Name _____   Date _____

STAGE EXPECTATIONS

On Our Way to English Grade 5	①	②	③	④	⑤
Content Area Knowledge Language Practice Game, Skills Masters, pages 38–39 How does the student demonstrate a knowledge of aspects of U.S. government?	Puts card in the appropriate section, sometimes naming the item. ☐ Yes ☐ Not yet	Puts card in the appropriate section, usually naming the item. ☐ Yes ☐ Not yet	Puts card in the appropriate section and uses appropriate language, such as *We have laws.* ☐ Yes ☐ Not yet	Puts card in the appropriate section and says two complete sentences with appropriate vocabulary, such as *We have a Supreme Court. It has justices.* ☐ Yes ☐ Not yet	
Social Language Function Express Obligation, Thematic Teacher's Guide, page 102 How does the student respond during the lesson?			Participates by supplying phrases or approximate sentences, such as *I should brush teeth.* ☐ Yes ☐ Not yet	Uses complete sentences, such as *Good citizens should vote.* ☐ Yes ☐ Not yet	
Academic Discussion Strategy Add to Someone's Comments, Thematic Teacher's Guide, page 90 How does the student respond during the lesson?			Adds to class comments, using simple sentences such as *I add to what Roberto says.* ☐ Yes ☐ Not yet	Adds to someone's comments using complete sentences, such as *I want to add that the president can veto any law that Congress makes.* ☐ Yes ☐ Not yet	
Anthology Retelling Thematic Teacher's Guide, pp. 108–113 Have each student use the back flap to retell the main selection. How does the student retell the selection?	Uses the web to point to the three branches of government in order. ☐ Yes ☐ Not yet	Points to the pictures representing each branch of government and uses a few words to describe each. ☐ Yes ☐ Not yet	Retells using longer phrases or simple sentences. ☐ Yes ☐ Not yet	Retells using complete sentences in connected discourse with few errors. ☐ Yes ☐ Not yet	Retells using language similar to native English-speaking peers. ☐ Yes ☐ Not yet
Open-Ended Oral Language Assessment, page A21 Use the student's responses to the illustration to reassess the student's Stage of Language Acquisition.	☐ **STAGE ①** Uses few or no words; gestures or points.	☐ **STAGE ②** Uses words or short phrases.	☐ **STAGE ③** Uses phrases and simple sentences.	☐ **STAGE ④** Uses sentences in connected discourse.	☐ **STAGE ⑤** Uses language comparable to native-speaking peers.

Open-Ended Oral Language Assessment

Reassess students' Language Acquisition Stages. Begin with an open-ended prompt like the first one below. If students are unable to respond, intervene with increasingly directed prompts, such as the second and third ones below.

What can you tell me about this picture?

What sounds can these people hear?

I see a barking dog. What else is making a sound?

Assessment Directions: Copy this form for each student and place the completed form in the student's portfolio. Locate the student's Language Acquisition Stage for each of the first four activities and assess his or her performance during the unit according to expectations for that Stage. For the Class Collection retelling, pull students to retell the main selection during end-of-unit assessment time. Use the Open-Ended Oral Language Assessment to reassess students' Language Acquisition Stages with one-fourth of your students for each unit, using the back side of the sheet to take notes. For more guidance on assessment, see the Assessment Handbook or the ELL Assessment Kit.

Unit 3 Assessment

Name _____   Date _____

STAGE EXPECTATIONS

On Our Way to English Grade 5	❶	❷	❸	❹	❺
Content Area Knowledge Language Practice Game, Skills Masters, page 66–67 How does the student demonstrate knowledge of sounds that can be heard in the city?	Places game markers in appropriate sections and sometimes names the pictured items. ☐ Yes ☐ Not yet	Places game markers in appropriate sections and usually names the pictured items. ☐ Yes ☐ Not yet	Places game markers in appropriate sections and uses appropriate language, such as *I hear siren.* ☐ Yes ☐ Not yet	Places game markers in appropriate sections and says a complete sentence, such as *I hear a siren when the fire truck comes.* ☐ Yes ☐ Not yet	
Social Language Function Express Feelings and Needs, Thematic Teacher's Guide, page 160 How does the student respond during the lesson?	Expresses feelings and needs with facial expressions and basic words, such as *happy or help* as they are able. ☐ Yes ☐ Not yet	Expresses feelings and needs with facial expressions and basic words, such as *happy or help* as they are able. ☐ Yes ☐ Not yet	Expresses feelings and needs in phrases, such as *feel happy or need help.* ☐ Yes ☐ Not yet	Expresses feelings and needs in sentences, such as *I feel happy when I hear music.* or *I need to call my mom so she knows I will be late.* ☐ Yes ☐ Not yet	
Academic Discussion Strategy Ask for an Opinion or Idea, Thematic Teacher's Guide, page 148 How does the student respond during the lesson?		Asks for an opinion using words or phrases, such as *Your idea, Hector?* ☐ Yes ☐ Not yet	Asks for an opinion using words or phrases, such as *Your idea, Hector?* ☐ Yes ☐ Not yet	Asks for an opinion using complete sentences, such as *What do you think, Soohee?* ☐ Yes ☐ Not yet	
Anthology Retelling Thematic Teacher's Guide, pp. 166–171 Have each student use the back flap to retell the main selection. How does the student retell the selection?	Uses the sequence organizer to point to the pictures in chronological order. ☐ Yes ☐ Not yet	Points to the pictures in chronological order and uses a few words. ☐ Yes ☐ Not yet	Retells using longer phrases or simple sentences. ☐ Yes ☐ Not yet	Retells using complete sentences in connected discourse with few errors. ☐ Yes ☐ Not yet	Retells using story language similar to native English-speaking peers. ☐ Yes ☐ Not yet
Open-Ended Oral Language Assessment, page A23 Use the student's responses to the illustration to reassess the student's Stage of Language Acquisition.	☐ STAGE ❶ Uses few or no words; gestures or points.	☐ STAGE ❷ Uses words or short phrases.	☐ STAGE ❸ Uses phrases and simple sentences.	☐ STAGE ❹ Uses sentences in connected discourse.	☐ STAGE ❺ Uses language comparable to native-speaking peers.

Open-Ended Oral Language Assessment

Reassess students' Language Acquisition Stages. Begin with an open-ended prompt like the first one below. If students are unable to respond, intervene with increasingly directed prompts, such as the second and third ones below.

What can you tell me about this picture?

What sea life do you see?

I see a shark. What sea life do you see?

Assessment Directions: Copy this form for each student and place the completed form in the student's portfolio. Locate the student's Language Acquisition Stage for each of the first four activities and assess his or her performance during the unit according to expectations for that Stage. For the Class Collection retelling, pull students to retell the main selection during end-of-unit assessment time. Use the Open-Ended Oral Language Assessment to reassess students' Language Acquisition Stages with one-fourth of your students for each unit, using the back side of the sheet to take notes. For more guidance on assessment, see the Assessment Handbook or the ELL Assessment Kit.

Unit 4 Assessment

Name _____ Date _____

On Our Way to English Grade 5

	STAGE EXPECTATIONS				
	1	**2**	**3**	**4**	**5**
Content Area Knowledge Language Practice Game, Skills Masters, pages 94–95 How does the student demonstrate knowledge of life in the ocean?	Puts game marker on the appropriate section of the game board, sometimes naming the item. ☐ Yes ☐ Not yet	Puts game marker on the appropriate section of the game board, usually naming the item. ☐ Yes ☐ Not yet	Puts game marker on the appropriate section of the game board and uses the sentence pattern ____ live in the ocean. ☐ Yes ☐ Not yet	Puts game marker on the appropriate section of the game board and says complete sentences with appropriate vocabulary, such as *The octopus lives in the ocean. It has eight arms.* ☐ Yes ☐ Not yet	
Social Language Function Express Likes and Dislikes, Thematic Teacher's Guide, page 218 How does the student respond during the lesson?	Expresses likes and dislikes by nodding and shaking head. ☐ Yes ☐ Not yet	Expresses likes and dislikes with phrases, such as *like chicken.* ☐ Yes ☐ Not yet	Expresses likes and dislikes with phrases, such as *I like chicken.* ☐ Yes ☐ Not yet	Expresses likes and dislikes in complete sentences, such as *I like clams. I don't like mussels.* ☐ Yes ☐ Not yet	
Academic Discussion Strategy Agree and Disagree, Thematic Teacher's Guide, page 206 How does the student respond during the lesson?		Agrees and disagrees using words or phrases, such as *I agree* or *I disagree.* ☐ Yes ☐ Not yet	Agrees and disagrees using words or phrases, such as *I agree* or *I disagree.* ☐ Yes ☐ Not yet	Agrees and disagrees using sentences, such as *I totally agree with Dana because . . .* or *Ricky has a point, but I have a completely different opinion about that.* ☐ Yes ☐ Not yet	
Anthology Retelling Thematic Teacher's Guide, pp. 224–229 Have each student use the back flap to retell the main selection. How does the student retell the selection?	Uses the chart to point to the pictures in correct succession. ☐ Yes ☐ Not yet	Points to the pictures in correct succession and uses a few words to describe them. ☐ Yes ☐ Not yet	Retells using longer phrases or simple sentences. ☐ Yes ☐ Not yet	Retells using complete sentences in connected discourse with few errors. ☐ Yes ☐ Not yet	Retells using language similar to native English-speaking peers. ☐ Yes ☐ Not yet
Open-Ended Oral Language Assessment, page A25 Use the student's responses to the illustration to reassess the student's Stage of Language Acquisition.	☐ **STAGE ①** Uses few or no words; gestures or points.	☐ **STAGE ②** Uses words or short phrases.	☐ **STAGE ③** Uses phrases and simple sentences.	☐ **STAGE ④** Uses sentences in connected discourse.	☐ **STAGE ⑤** Uses language comparable to native-speaking peers.

Open-Ended Oral Language Assessment

Reassess students' Language Acquisition Stages. Begin with an open-ended prompt like the first one below. If students are unable to respond, intervene with increasingly directed prompts, such as the second and third ones below.

What can you tell me about this picture?

How do you see the nation growing?

I see people exploring. How do you see the nation growing?

Assessment Directions: Copy this form for each student and place the completed form in the student's portfolio. Locate the student's Language Acquisition Stage for each of the first four activities and assess his or her performance during the unit according to expectations for that Stage. For the Class Collection retelling, pull students to retell the main selection during end-of-unit assessment time. Use the Open-Ended Oral Language Assessment to reassess students' Language Acquisition Stages with one-fourth of your students for each unit, using the back side of the sheet to take notes. For more guidance on assessment, see the Assessment Handbook or the ELL Assessment Kit.

Name _____ **Date** _____

Unit 5 Assessment

On Our Way to English Grade 5

STAGE EXPECTATIONS

	❶	❷	❸	❹	❺
Content Area Knowledge Language Practice Game, Skills Masters, pages 120–121 How does the student demonstrate a knowledge about who and what went west?	Moves game marker to appropriate space, sometimes naming the item. ☐ Yes ☐ Not yet	Moves game marker to appropriate space, usually naming the item. ☐ Yes ☐ Not yet	Moves game marker to appropriate space and uses appropriate language, e.g., *coach went West.* ☐ Yes ☐ Not yet	Says complete sentences with appropriate vocabulary, e.g., *Wagons went West. They drove on trails.* ☐ Yes ☐ Not yet	
Social Language Function Use Appropriate Register, Thematic Teacher's Guide, page 276 How does the student respond during the lesson?			Uses formal and informal register in the appropriate situation. ☐ Yes ☐ Not yet	Uses formal and informal register in the appropriate situation such as *The topic of my presentation is . . .* when presenting to the class. ☐ Yes ☐ Not yet	
Academic Discussion Strategy Ask for Evidence, Thematic Teacher's Guide, page 264 How does the student respond during the lesson?			Asks for evidence, using words or phrases, such as *How you know?* ☐ Yes ☐ Not yet	Asks for evidence, using complete sentences, such as *Can you show me which part of the text tells you that early settlers had a hard time traveling?* ☐ Yes ☐ Not yet	
Anthology Retelling? Thematic Teacher's Guide, pp. 282–287 Have each student use the back flap to retell the main selection. How does the student retell the selection?	Uses the time line to point to the pictures in the correct succession. ☐ Yes ☐ Not yet	Points to the pictures in the correct succession and uses a few words. ☐ Yes ☐ Not yet	Retells using longer phrases or simple sentences. ☐ Yes ☐ Not yet	Retells using complete sentences in connected discourse with few errors. ☐ Yes ☐ Not yet	Retells using language similar to native English-speaking peers. ☐ Yes ☐ Not yet
Open-Ended Oral Language Assessment, page A27 Use the student's responses to the illustration to reassess the student's Stage of Language Acquisition.	☐ **STAGE ❶** Uses few or no words; gestures or points.	☐ **STAGE ❷** Uses words or short phrases.	☐ **STAGE ❸** Uses phrases and simple sentences.	☐ **STAGE ❹** Uses sentences in connected discourse.	☐ **STAGE ❺** Uses language comparable to native-speaking peers.

A28

Thematic Unit 5

A Growing Nation

Open-Ended Oral Language Assessment

Reassess students' Language Acquisition Stages. Begin with an open-ended prompt like the first one below. If students are unable to respond, intervene with increasingly directed prompts, such as the second and third ones below.

What can you tell me about this picture?

What technology do you see?

I see a CD player. What technology do you see?

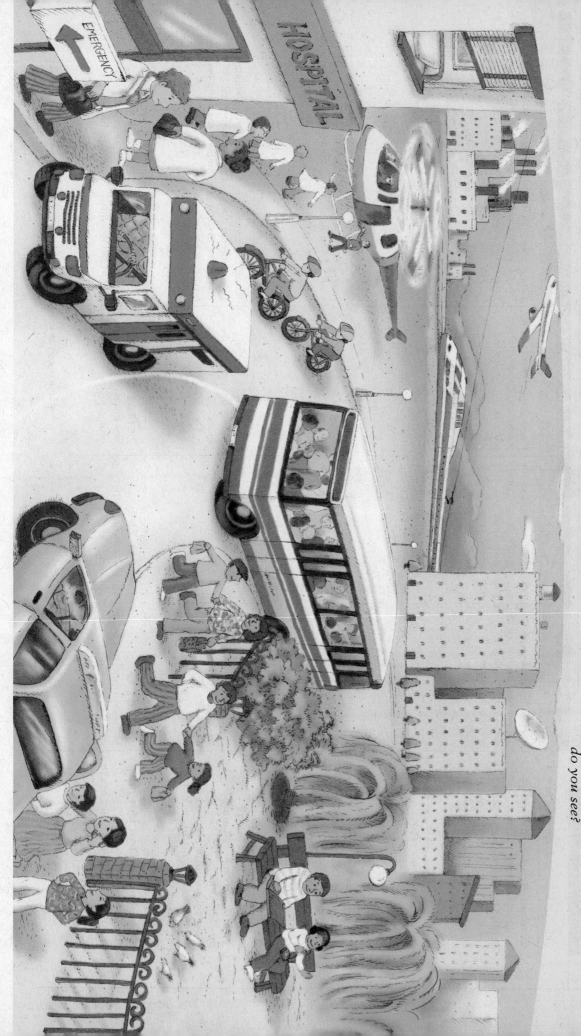

Assessment Directions: Copy this form for each student and place the completed form in the student's portfolio. Locate the student's Language Acquisition Stage for each of the first four activities and assess his or her performance during the unit according to expectations for that Stage. For the Class Collection retelling, pull students to retell the main selection during end-of-unit assessment time. Use the Open-Ended Oral Language Assessment to reassess students' Language Acquisition Stages with one-fourth of your students for each unit, using the back side of the sheet to take notes. For more guidance on assessment, see the Assessment Handbook or the ELL Assessment Kit.

Name _____ **Date** _____

Unit 6 Assessment

On Our Way to English Grade 5

STAGE EXPECTATIONS

	❶	❷	❸	❹	❺
Content Area Knowledge Language Practice Game, Skills Masters, pages 147–148. How does the student demonstrate knowledge of inventions and technology?	Puts game markers in the appropriate section of the game board, usually naming the item. ☐ Yes ☐ Not yet	Puts game markers in the appropriate section of the game board, usually naming the item. ☐ Yes ☐ Not yet	Places game markers correctly, using the sentence pattern ____ helps me. ☐ Yes ☐ Not yet	Puts markers in the appropriate section of the game board, using the key sentence pattern followed by a prepositional phrase. ☐ Yes ☐ Not yet	
Social Language Function Give Instructions, Thematic Teacher's Guide, page 334. How does the student respond during the lesson?		Is able to give and follow instructions through demonstration and some words. ☐ Yes ☐ Not yet	Is able to give simple instructions, such as *Turn on the computer.* ☐ Yes ☐ Not yet	Is able to give complete and detailed instructions from start to finish, using complete sentences. ☐ Yes ☐ Not yet	
Academic Discussion Strategy Provide Evidence, Thematic Teacher's Guide, page 322. How does the student respond during the lesson?			Is able to provide evidence from the text, using simple language, such as *says here.* ☐ Yes ☐ Not yet	Is able to provide evidence using complete sentences, such as *I know that because electric cars can help cut down on pollution.* ☐ Yes ☐ Not yet	
Anthology Retelling? Thematic Teacher's Guide, pp. 340–345. Have each student use the back flap to retell the main selection. How does the student retell the selection?	Uses the flow chart to point to the pictures in the correct succession. ☐ Yes ☐ Not yet	Points to the pictures in the correct succession and uses a few words. ☐ Yes ☐ Not yet	Retells, using longer phrases or simple sentences. ☐ Yes ☐ Not yet	Retells, using complete sentences in connected discourse with few errors. ☐ Yes ☐ Not yet	Retells, using language similar to native English-speaking peers. ☐ Yes ☐ Not yet
Open-Ended Oral Language Assessment, page A29 Use the student's responses to the illustration to reassess the student's Stage of Language Acquisition.	☐ **STAGE ❶** Uses few or no words; gestures or points.	☐ **STAGE ❷** Uses words or short phrases.	☐ **STAGE ❸** Uses phrases and simple sentences.	☐ **STAGE ❹** Uses sentences in connected discourse.	☐ **STAGE ❺** Uses language comparable to native-speaking peers.

Open-Ended Oral Language Assessment

Reassess students' Language Acquisition Stages. Begin with an open-ended prompt like the first one below. If students are unable to respond, intervene with increasingly directed prompts, such as the second and third ones below.

What can you tell me about this picture?

What things in space do you see?

I see the moon. What things in space do you see?

Assessment Directions: Copy this form for each student and place the completed form in the student's portfolio. Locate the student's Language Acquisition Stage for each of the first four activities and assess his or her performance during the unit according to expectations for that Stage. For the Class Collection Retelling, pull students to retell the main selection during end-of-unit assessment time. Use the Open-Ended Oral Language Assessment to reassess students' Language Acquisition Stages with one-fourth of your students for each unit, using the back side of the sheet to take notes. For more guidance on assessment, see the Assessment Handbook or the ELL Assessment Kit.

Name _____ **Date** _____

Unit 7 Assessment

On Our Way to English Grade 5

	STAGE EXPECTATIONS				
	1	**2**	**3**	**4**	**5**
Content Area Knowledge Language Practice Game, Skills Masters, pages 172–173 How does the student demonstrate knowledge of planets moving around the sun?	Places game markers on appropriate spaces, sometimes naming the planets. ☐ Yes ☐ Not yet	Places game markers on appropriate spaces, usually naming the planets. ☐ Yes ☐ Not yet	Uses appropriate language, such as Mars moves around sun. ☐ Yes ☐ Not yet	Uses appropriate language, such as Mars moves around the sun and makes a comparison, such as It is closer to the sun than Pluto. ☐ Yes ☐ Not yet	
Social Language Function Negotiate, Thematic Teacher's Guide, page 392 How does the student respond during the lesson?			Negotiates plans, such as Read first? OK? ☐ Yes ☐ Not yet	Negotiates plans, such as *I want to read this book first. Is that OK?* ☐ Yes ☐ Not yet	
Academic Discussion Strategy Ask for Explanations, Thematic Teacher's Guide, page 380 How does the student respond during the lesson?		Asks for explanations, using single words or phrases, such as *Why?* or *Explain again.* ☐ Yes ☐ Not yet	Asks for explanations, using single words or phrases, such as *Why?* or *Explain again.*	Asks for explanations, using complete sentences, such as *That does not make sense because our books do not float. Can you explain that again?* ☐ Yes ☐ Not yet	
Anthology Retelling? Thematic Teacher's Guide, pp. 398–403 Have each student use the back flap to retell the main selection. How does the student retell the selection?	Uses the cause-and-effect organizer to point to the pictures relating cause to effects. ☐ Yes ☐ Not yet	Points to the pictures relating cause and effects and uses a few words. ☐ Yes ☐ Not yet	Retells, using longer phrases or simple sentences. ☐ Yes ☐ Not yet	Retells, using complete sentences in connected discourse with few errors. ☐ Yes ☐ Not yet	Retells, using language similar to native English-speaking peers. ☐ Yes ☐ Not yet
Open-Ended Oral Language Assessment, page A31 Use the student's responses to the illustration to reassess the student's Stage of Language Acquisition.	☐ **STAGE ❶** Uses few or no words; gestures or points.	☐ **STAGE ❷** Uses words or short phrases.	☐ **STAGE ❸** Uses phrases and simple sentences.	☐ **STAGE ❹** Uses sentences in connected discourse.	☐ **STAGE ❺** Uses language comparble to native-speaking peers.

A32

Thematic Unit 7

Earth, Moon, and Sun

Open-Ended Oral Language Assessment

Reassess students' Language Acquisition Stages. Begin with an open-ended prompt like the first one below. If students are unable to respond, intervene with increasingly directed prompts, such as the second and third ones below.

What can you tell me about this picture?

What life systems do you see?

I see a skeleton. What life systems do you see?

A33

Assessment Directions: Copy this form for each student and place the completed form in the student's portfolio. Locate the student's Language Acquisition Stage for each of the first four activities and assess his or her performance during the unit according to expectations for that Stage. For the Class Collection retelling, pull students to retell the main selection during end-of-unit assessment time. Use the Open-Ended Oral Language Assessment to reassess students' Language Acquisition Stages with one-fourth of your students for each unit, using the back side of the sheet to take notes. For more guidance on assessment, see the Assessment Handbook or the ELL Assessment Kit.

Name _____   **Date** _____

Unit 8 Assessment

STAGE EXPECTATIONS

On Our Way to English Grade 5	①	②	③	④	⑤
Content Area Knowledge Language Practice Game, Skills Masters, pages 198–199 How does the student demonstrate a knowledge of human organs?	Puts a marker on the appropriate section of the game board and sometimes says the name of the organ. ☐ Yes ☐ Not yet	Puts a marker on the appropriate section of the game board and usually says the name of the organ. ☐ Yes ☐ Not yet	Puts a marker on the appropriate section and uses the pattern We have _____ in our bodies. ☐ Yes ☐ Not yet	Puts a marker on the appropriate section of the game board while identifying and describing the function of the corresponding organ, e.g., We have a brain in our bodies. It helps us think. ☐ Yes ☐ Not yet	
Social Language Function Warn, Thematic Teacher's Guide, page 450 How does the student respond during the lesson?	Demonstrates, through gestures, warnings given by classmates. ☐ Yes ☐ Not yet		Gives simple warnings, such as *Stop!* or *Watch out!* ☐ Yes ☐ Not yet	Gives complete warnings with consequences for not following the warning, such as *Always look both ways before crossing the street so that you do not get hit by a car.* ☐ Yes ☐ Not yet	
Academic Discussion Strategy Provide Explanations, Thematic Teacher's Guide, page 438 How does the student respond during the lesson?			Offers explanations, using simple sentences, such as *Book says leaves make plant food.* ☐ Yes ☐ Not yet	Gives explanations along with reasons, such as *Based on the text, I think the when we exercise, we make our hearts and other muscles stronger.* ☐ Yes ☐ Not yet	
Anthology Retelling? Thematic Teacher's Guide, pp. 456–461 Have each student use the back flap to retell the main selection. How does the student retell the selection?	Points to causes and related effects in the chart. ☐ Yes ☐ Not yet	Points to causes and effects, using a few words to describe each. ☐ Yes ☐ Not yet	Retells, using longer phrases or simple sentences. ☐ Yes ☐ Not yet	Retells, using complete sentences in connected discourse with few errors. ☐ Yes ☐ Not yet	Retells, using language similar to native-speaking peers. ☐ Yes ☐ Not yet
Open-Ended Oral Language Assessment, page A33 Use the student's responses to the illustration to reassess the student's Stage of Language Acquisition.	☐ **STAGE ①** Uses few or no words; gestures or points.	☐ **STAGE ②** Uses words or short phrases.	☐ **STAGE ③** Uses phrases and simple sentences.	☐ **STAGE ④** Uses sentences in connected discourse.	☐ **STAGE ⑤** Uses language comparable to native-speaking peers.

© 2010 Rigby®, an imprint of HMH Supplemental Publishers Inc. All rights reserved.

134

Thematic Unit 8

Pulse of Life